Are We Having Fun Yet?

Wry Slices Of Life

Have fun!

T. Smith

By
Tim Smith

2003

Parkway Publishers, Inc.
Boone, North Carolina

Copyright 2003 by Timothy M. Smith

All Rights Reserved

Available from:
Parkway Publishers, Inc.
P. O. Box 3678
Boone, North Carolina 28607
Telephone/Facsimile: (828) 265-3993

www.parkwaypublishers.com

Library of Congress Cataloging in Publication Data

Smith, Tim, 1954 Nov. 1-
Are we having fun yet? : wry slices of life / by Tim Smith.
p. cm.
ISBN 1-887905-80-4
1. Family—Humor. 2. Family life—Humor. I. Title.

PN6231.F3S65 2004
814'.6—dc22
2003022431

Editing, Layout and Book Design: Julie Shissler
Cover Design: Aaron Burleson, Spokesmedia

Part I – Kid's Stuff

Part II –The Nature of Things

Part III - Learning Life's Lessons

Part IV - Fun and Games

Part V - Getting Older

for Freda Belle, who always believed

*I am indebted to many people for helping make this a reality:
Phil and Laura Smith, David and Babette Ford, Rao Aluri,
Julie Shissler, Rachel Rivers-Coffey, and Betty Gordon, to
name a few. Thanks so very much.*

*And last but not least, thanks to Larson and Kelsey
for all the fun.*

Part I

Kid Stuff

1 - Off To School

I remember the day I lost my son.

Oh, I don't mean he'd been carelessly misplaced; it was the day he started school. It was a day I couldn't help but feel was the end of an era.

Then again, maybe I'm crazy. It takes a certain amount of insanity to have children, which makes it all the more curious that parenthood is one of the few things the government hasn't decreed is against the law. And it doesn't take much to push a parent over the edge; an introduction to the public education system is more than enough.

The contradictions of parenthood are enough to drive you nuts, too. Kids clutch at you like you are life itself, and you never have a minute completely to yourself. Yet as my first-born prepared to go off to school I found it hard to let go even a little, afraid that small hand would never want to hold mine again.

Besides, I'm losing authority. Control. Influence. Raw, unadulterated power.

One of the nice things about being a dad is the semblance of authority. At home you're the Big Cheese, Mr. Big - dad with a capital "D." Plus, you're the resident expert on everything; you have the answer to any question, and believe me, 5-year-olds have plenty of them. Your word is gospel, unless of course Mom says otherwise. You can get a kid to believe anything - until he starts school and is corrupted by the insidious influences of the real world.

I wonder if he would still believe me when I tell him as he morosely picks at a sickly green stalk lying limply on his plate at the dinner table that broccoli is the stuff by which alien beings from all parts of the galaxy - and possibly beyond - power their space craft and they may accidentally beam him up trying to get his plateful if he doesn't get to gobbling, when his teachers will soon be telling him that the universe as he knows it is confined to the four cheery walls of his classroom?

And where will he receive his geopolitical views on life from now on? Will he believe the sophisticated, reasoned analyses offered up by his father, such as war is the uttermost failure of humankind's efforts, or the puerile drivel of his peers, who declaim on how war is pretty neat stuff because you get to blast bad guys in the guts?

Already I have had to fight the ravenous consumerism instilled in him by television - "Let's buy this, Dad; all you have to do is call this toll-free number that I've memorized even though I can't remember to brush my teeth every morning" - and am being assaulted by the infamous "not" craze: "Dad, I think the dog ate your wallet - NOT!!! Ha, ha, ha!"

This is the trickle-down theory of popular culture at work; this stupid fad originated, I believe, a couple of years ago among the smart teen set, no doubt in California where chowderheadedness is often mistaken for wit, and is only now settling down to its true constituency, the kindergarten crowd.

But back to school. How do I tell him of what lies ahead? How do I tell him of my worries and concerns? What if he's bored? What if he doesn't like his teacher? What if he can't make new friends? What if he can't make a date for the big kindergarten dance?

How to I tell him it's all teeter-totter time now, but algebra and biology lab lurk down the hall? School is an endless progression from childhood to adulthood, with the horrors of teenhood just around the corner: An insatiable appetite for money, driving MY car, youthful rebellion against parental controls, raging hormones, unfathomable music, and bizarre tastes in clothes.

But how do you tell a child not to grow up? Life's an adventure when you're young, and you face each day not with gloomy regrets but with bright expectations.

I watch my son go off to school and embark upon life's long journey. I'll be with him every step of the way, but part of me, I fear, will have been left behind forever.

2 - Breakfast Is No Picnic

If it's morning at my house, it must be time for the Battle of the Breakfast Table.

Who says war is glamorous? I can testify firsthand that it is brutish and ugly. Especially with cold cereal.

It is a parental duty to muster all the energy available on a cold, dreary morning while trying not to think about the day looming ahead with its unending stream of problems and headaches in order to greet your impressionable offspring with a cheery smile and a hearty "good morning!" even if all you really feel like doing is going back to bed.

It is at this time the opening salvo is fired: "What do you guys want for breakfast?"

Parents know that all children suffer from selective hearing impairment, so you automatically repeat this type of question three times before you expect any sort of response. In this case, the response comes in the form of a blank stare, as though I had just informed my children that we were moving to Tanzania.

"How about some cereal?" I suggest.

"No," I am told – not unexpectedly, since children rarely accept the first suggestion.

"Toast?

They look at each other. No, they agree, that won't do.

"Waffles?"

Perhaps. "What else is there?" they want to know.

I stifle the impulse to tell them that the choices are the same as yesterday and the day before. "Fruit," I offer instead. "It's good for you. You need to eat some fruit."

Maybe. They'll take it under consideration. Meanwhile, could they take in a little TV?

"No. No TV. We have to get ready. It's getting late. We need to eat."

"How about you just fix us a surprise, Dad?"

A surprise. "Great," I say, tight-lipped. "No problem."

Minutes later, the cantaloupe is cut, the cereal is in the bowls, orange juice is in their glasses, and the toast is browned and buttered and sliced into cute little triangles just the way they like.

"OK, kids, breakfast is ready!"

They, of course, are not. They are fighting for position in front of the heater.

"He pushed me, Daddy!" my daughter exclaims, firing the first shot.

"No, I didn't," my son retorts indignantly. "I got here first, and she was in the way."

I try not to wrap my mind around this form of logic this early in the day. "Let's just eat, shall we?"

"But, Dad, she touched me!"

"Did not!"

"Did, too!"

They are dragged to the table.

"Ewwww. I don't want this," my daughter informs me.

"What's wrong with it?"

"That's not what I wanted. I wanted a Pop Tart."

"Well, you didn't say you wanted a Pop Tart. You said you wanted a surprise. This is a surprise. A nice surprise. Now get to eating. My cereal is getting soggy."

She promptly bursts into tears, traumatized for life, no doubt, by my heartless cruelty. I sigh. I look for help to my wife, who is making herself busy fixing their lunches. Actually, she's been in the kitchen for awhile, now, making those lunches. Must be quite a smorgasbord she's laying on for the kids.

"Honey, don't you want to come eat with us?" I call out hopefully.

"I'm busy," she calls back. "Fixing their lunches."

I sigh again. It's lonely at the front. "Calm down," I tell my sobbing daughter. "You eat some of that, and I'll fix you a Pop Tart. OK?" Call it a tactical retreat.

"But I don't want a Pop Tart," she sniffs. "I want a doughnut."

I decide on an unseemly withdrawal, and take my cereal into the kitchen to eat. I look at the clock; the morning is 20 minutes old. It's going to be a longer day than I had initially suspected. A moment later, I am recalled to the front.

"Dad, she's bothering me," my son informs me.

"What's she doing now?"

"She showed me her food."

"What's wrong with that?"

"It was in her mouth."

4

I rub my eyes with fatigue. "Guys, just go get dressed, OK?" I survey the battlefield, which is littered with odd scraps of crust, small mounds of butter, bits of fruit, and a doughnut ringed with teeth marks from a tiny mouth.

"Daddy?"

I turn around to look at my daughter, who has stopped on her way upstairs.

"Yes, sweetie," I say.

"Can we go out for supper?"

3 - *Legislating Away Childish Problems*

It's been another long day, and I haven't even left the house yet.

There are many mornings that I find myself being less a parent and more an early-morning referee.

The problem today is breathtaking in scale: My daughter is singing a silly little tune, and it's driving her brother mad with rage.

"Stop it!" he shrieks.

Sensing that he is somewhat bothered by her musical expression, she does what any child would do: She follows him around the house warbling away.

I ask her to cease and desist. Or at least to remove herself from his vicinity.

She backs off a few steps.

Moments later I hear a scream from the bathroom. I rush in, imagining all sorts of watery troubles. My son is trying to brush his teeth and is near tears.

"She's LOOKING at me," he sobs in response to my wordless inquiry.

"And..." I prompt.

"And she's still singing."

I sigh. This, I muse, must be how political divisions are born.

I can see this one day becoming a major political issue of the land. Powerful members of Congress, harking back to their troubled home lives filled with spiteful siblings, will rail against the evils of youthful singing.

"A constitutional amendment," they will cry, "outlawing singing among juveniles is the only way to instill a sense of decency, morality and respect in today's youth. Shameless singing encourages irresponsibility, disrespect of authority and, probably, lascivious behavior. Besides, it's the only way we'll get our sisters to shut up."

It wouldn't take much for the childhood singing ban bandwagon to get rolling. Jumping aboard would be the large and powerful Poked and Prodded crowd. You know, the ones who as children were always yelling, "Don't TOUCH me again!"

And then the early bed-timers would chime in, grousing even after all these years how they had to turn in earlier than their older brothers and sisters, thereby missing "Bonanza" in its prime. Surely a law is needed to make bedtime uniform for all children.

Let's not forget the victims of mimicry. Cruel and unusual punishment for any child it is to be subjected to a sibling echoing every word and aping every gesture. As the drive for this childhood behavior amendment picked up steam, parents across the country would be looking at each other, nodding their heads, and thinking, "Yes, this makes sense. We can tell our kids that it really is against the law to talk with your mouth full of food."

Amendment opponents, most likely muttering about minor details such as the First Amendment - which, by the way, says nothing about the right to sing - would be roundly booed off the public stage. After all, peace in the home is at stake here, so surely the ends justify the means in this case.

It's a good thing, however, that we're civilized in this country. In other lands, childhood problems could lead to more violent conflicts.

It's not hard to see, for instance, that persecution complexes in Third World dictators which inspire them to invade their neighbors with massive armies intent on rampant destruction were caused primarily by lost television privileges at an early age, with this punitive action brought on by tormenting their sisters with tales of monsters under the bed.

Yes, in America we live by the rules of law, so that every problem, no matter how childish, can be legislated away without a violent outcome.

Now, about that constitutional amendment requiring children to been seen and not heard...

4 - Fighting the Fashion Wars

I hear the rumble from the battlefield all the way in the kitchen.

It makes me ponder the eternal question of fatherhood: Should I be brave and gallantly rush off to the front lines, or play the sniveling coward and enjoy the comforts back here behind the lines.

Stupidity wins. I sigh as I trudge up the stairs. I pass my wife, who is in quick retreat from the horrors of the combat zone.

"What's the problem?" I ask brightly. I notice what appears to be smoke pouring from her ears. Fire is in her eye. Astutely, I take these as bad signs.

"Agh!" she sputters.

"Agh?" I respond politely.

"Your daughter…" she begins. Uh oh, I think as my heart sinks, this is bad: She's already disowned her and it's not yet 8 o'clock in the morning.

"Yes? What about our lovely, adorable child?"

She glares at me. "I can't take it anymore," she tells me. "I just can't."

"What's that, dear?" I soothe.

"Her clothes. She asks me to help her pick out something for school, and when I go in there and suggest something she tells me she doesn't want any help. All those clothes I bought her … she says she doesn't like them anymore. She's worn them once! Once! That's it. I'm not buying her any more clothes, ever again. Let her buy her own clothes."

"She's 8 years old, dear," I feel compelled to point out.

"I don't care. She can spend what little money she does have and buy her own clothes."

I sigh. I debate the wisdom of pointing out that this whole clothes business might just be a girl thing. I mean, guys just aren't quite as particular about what they wear. I wasn't all that picky as a kid, and for years my son has been wearing pretty much any old thing. I'm all for equality of the sexes, but let's be realistic: Most clotheshorses are of the feminine persuasion.

Years of marital experience tell me that I should probably keep my thoughts on gender characteristics to myself for the time being.

Time to send in the cavalry. I march up the stairs prepared to attack. My daughter is sitting on her bed in her pajamas, weeping.

"What's up?" I ask, reconnoitering the territory.

"Nothing," she manages to say through her tears.

"Nothing?" I say, dubiously.

"Well," her voice quavers, "Mom's being mean to me."

"Oh?" I say. "And how is she being mean?"

"She won't help me pick out my clothes for school." This is followed by another burst of tears.

"Hmmmm," I say. "Are you sure Mom was being mean or was it you just didn't like what she picked out?"

"Dad, she never lets me wear what I want."

"Oh, come now. What is it you want to wear?"

She prods a pile of clothes with her toe. "That."

"Honey, it's 20 degrees outside. Don't you think you might be a bit cold wearing shorts and a T-shirt?"

"No. I'm always hot at school."

"I know, baby, but you'll be cold getting there. How about we pick out something else?"

"OK."

I'm feeling smug now. The battle's half-won. I want to go get my wife and show her how to reason with an 8-year-old.

"How about this?" she asks, holding up a tiny scrap of fabric.

I frown. "I don't think they allow you to wear things like that to school. How about a nice pair of sweats and a sweatshirt?"

"Daaaaaad," she wails, throwing herself back on her bed.

"What? What is it? What'd I do?"

"I'll look like a dork in that," she says.

"Well, how about these jeans and this shirt?"

"Duh, Dad, like they don't even match."

I'm feeling that the tide of battle has turned. Suddenly, I'm on the defensive.

"Hmmm," I stall, rummaging in her closet. "How about a dress?"

"No, Dad," as though I'd suggested she shave her head.

"Well," I say, trying to keep the exasperation out of my voice, "what do you want to wear?"

"Anything," she says.

"Anything?"

"Anything that doesn't look dorky."

9

"And what might that be?

"I don't know. That's why I wanted Mom's help!"

She's bawling again. I debate whether to desert the field of battle now, or try one more assault. "Honey," I say sweetly, "how about some of these new clothes Mom bought you?"

"Dad, they all make me look ..."

"I know, I know. Dorky." I sigh again. As I survey the carnage, I contemplate a conditional surrender. "Tell you what, honey," I say, "wear these pants and I'll let you wear a T-shirt. But you have to wear a jacket."

"Dad! Do I have to?"

"Absolutely. I'm not sending you off to school when it's this cold without a jacket."

That settled, I head out the door, victory in my grasp. But she stops me dead in my tracks.

"Dad, my tennis shoes don't fit anymore."

"But, honey, we just got them. Are you sure they don't fit, or is it ... never mind. Just wear them."

"But Dad!" More tears are coming.

"Just wear them!" I yell, fleeing the battlefield before I manage to snatch defeat from the jaws of victory. I hear my wife chuckling somewhere. At least she's in a better mood now.

My son saunters downstairs a bit later. I look at his shoes. "Son," I say, "are your shoes tied?"

He gives me a pained expression. "Yes, Dad."

"Then why do they look so loose? They look like you could step right out of them."

"That's how I like them," he explains patiently, as if telling a 3-year-old that the sky is blue. "That's how people wear them today. That way you don't have to keep tying and untying them."

"Ah," I say in bewilderment while I nod knowingly.

My wife appears and surveys the situation. She tells our son to pull his pants up.

"Why?" he asks, perplexed.

"Because," I point out, "your underwear is showing."

"No, they're not," he protests in a tone of righteous indignation.

"Yes, they are. I can see them."

"No, you can't."

"Yes, I can."

"Where?"

"What do you mean, 'where'? There."

"I can't see them."

I sigh again. "Son, what is it with this baggy-pants-falling-off-the-butt fashion thing? Why do you guys think anyone wants to see your underwear? What's wrong with wearing a belt? Everyone at your school is wandering around with their pants halfway down their legs. What's that all about?"

"Dad, it's just how you wear pants."

"No, it isn't. In my day…" I stop, having heard what I just said. I hated it when my parents used to tell me how it was in their day. "Um, it used to be that we laughed at people who had their underwear showing. Usually it was fat guys whose pants were hanging way down, their jockey shorts were showing, and so was a half moon."

"Yeah, but I wear boxers," he retorts. "And my shirt hangs down over my pants."

I shake my head. "Well, if you're so hot to show off your boxers, why not start a new fad? Why not wear them outside your pants? Or on your head, like some kind of mod bandana?"

"Or how about this?" I ask, warming to the subject. Having heard my rants before, my son groans. "Why not wear your socks outside your shoes? I know; guys are always wearing their hats backwards – why not your clothes, too? Or pull your pants way up and have them belted around your armpits like that Urkel guy on the TV show."

"Is that what you guys did back in the old days?" he asks innocently.

"No, we wore … never mind what we wore."

"Oh, I know what you wore. I've seen all those black and white TV shows from way back when," he says smugly.

"See here," I say, trying not to let on how close to the mark he's hit. "When I was your age the TV shows were in color. Mostly."

"Yeah, but what about those clothes you wore? Huh?"

I think back to the fashions of the past. I wince. Bell-bottoms. Tie-dyed shirts. Nehru jackets. Things with fringes. Beads and bangles.

Of course, all that eventually gave way to the real world, with real clothes suitable for life as a functioning adult. My hand unconsciously rubs my neck as I think back to all the ties I have worn in my life. Who dreamed those things up, anyway? Who decided at some point in human history that stylish clothes should be uncomfortable? I mean, were all the fashion czars sitting around one day and one of them say, "Hey, here's a joke we can play. Let's tell all the men that they have to wrap a piece of colored cloth – no, no, wait, a real expensive piece of silk or something – around their neck and tie it on really tight so they choke. Ha, ha!"

After they've all stopped laughing, did another one say, "Wait, I've got another idea. Let's tell women that they should wear these tiny little shoes with a big spike on the heel so that they walk around on their tiptoes all day. Do you think they'd fall for that? I mean, after all, they went for panty hose."

My wandering mind returns to the here and now. My son is still grinning at me. I look at his shoes, at his pants hanging down, at his two layers of T-shirts. I sigh.

"Son," I say. "I see your point."

He chuckles.

"But let me ask you one thing." I pause. "Where's your jacket?"

5 - Let's Not Argue

Life sometimes seems like one long argument.

For me, the arguing begins as soon as I climb out of bed.

"Kids," I call into their rooms, "time to wake up."

"Mrrrrmph," I hear. I consider this response and decide it could loosely be translated as: "We hear you but are deciding to ignore you."

I go into my daughter's room. "Time to wake up, sweetie."

"I am," comes the muffled voice from under the covers.

"Then you need to get up."

"I am," the voice insists.

"No you're not. Get up means out of the bed. You're in the bed." Nothing like teaching a bit of logic to the kids early in the morning.

"I mean I'll get up," says the voice, confounding logic.

I move to her brother's room. "OK, son, rise and shine."

"I'm up, I'm up," he says from under his covers. I decide to leave it at that.

At the breakfast table, it's more of the same.

"C'mon, guys, eat up, we're running late."

"We are," they both chorus, although I refrain from pointing out that neither is actually chewing food since neither, technically, has put any food in their mouths in at least five minutes, clearly hoping that if they dawdle over breakfast for several hours then the demands of school will somehow simply disappear for the day.

"Well, finish up."

"We are."

I look at the food on their plates. I sigh.

"Well, then, go get ready."

They amble back to their rooms. Time passes.

"Guys, are you about ready?" I yell up the stairs.

"Yeah!" they yell back.

Years of experience as a professional cynic kick in. I head up the stairs. My son is watching "Sports Center" on his TV. He still has on his pajamas.

"Son," I say patiently, "you need to be getting ready for school."

"I am," he avows.

"You are?"

"Yes! I'm getting my clothes on!"

I look at him on the bed. I look at his clothes in his closet. I plunge ahead. "You are?"

He looks at me with the exasperation a teen reserves for those moments when realization strikes that his pitiable parent, once the source of all light and illumination in life, is clearly just another dim bulb.

"Yes. Just give me a minute."

I steel myself as I head to the next room. "Sweetie, are you about ready?"

My daughter is sitting on her bed, weeping. She, too, is in her pajamas.

I take a deep breath. "Let me guess …" I begin.

"I don't have anything to wear," she wails.

"Yes, you do."

"No, I don't."

"Sure you do. Your closet is full of stuff."

"No, it isn't."

"Yes, it is. Look."

"But I can't wear any of that."

"You can't?"

"No!"

"Why not?"

"I just can't!"

I ponder a logical response but come up empty. I decide to fall back on emergency measures. "I'll go get mom. She'll find something. In the meantime, go get your teeth brushed, OK?"

My son is downstairs.

"Are you ready?" I ask.

"Yep," he says smugly.

"You have all your stuff?"

"Yep."

"Where's your backpack?"

He looks around. "In my room."

"Don't you think you'll need it?"

He rolls his eyes. It is, of course, the parent's fault that the school requires that he bring home and take back books, papers, pencils, etc. He heads back upstairs.

I sigh again. Not for the first time I wonder how much boarding school would cost. At least then I'd only have to have the following conversation at holidays when they came home rather than after school every day of the week:

"Hi, kids, how was school?" I ask brightly as they roll in.

"Mmmmph."

"Really?" I reply. "That's good." I prepare myself for the next question. "Um, so, guys, do you have much homework?"

"No," they both respond.

"Really?" I wait a beat. "None at all?"

"Nope," my son responds. He waits two beats. "Except for math, of course."

"Of course," I reply helpfully. I wait patiently.

"And some spelling."

"Is that all?"

"Yep. Oh, and some vocabulary stuff. And I have to write this paper."

"Well, that doesn't sound like much," I lie. I turn toward my daughter. "And how about you?"

"I don't have any homework," she announces proudly.

"You're sure?"

"Well … there is this math sheet I need to finish. And this science test we're supposed to study for."

"You want some help studying for it?"

"Nah. We went over it in class."

"Yes, but don't you think you should go over it again?"

She looks at me as though I suggested she try eating raw worms for a snack. "Daddy," she says patiently, looking at the ceiling while my son stands there smirking. "I know it, OK?"

"What's the test on?"

"I don't know, something about energy and stuff."

"You don't know what the test is on exactly but you're sure you know the material, is that what you're telling me?"

"Well, yeah." She rolls her eyes – a trick she learned from her brother. Like, duh, Dad.

"C'mon, guys," I say. "Why do we have to argue about everything?"

"We don't," they say. Of course.

I look at the clock. Only six more hours until their bedtime. Or mine.

But then bedtime is almost as bad as the morning routine. Children are genetically engineered to never get ready for bed on their own, and they never seem to be able to tell time at night.

"Time for bed," I'll tell my daughter as I poke my head into her room.

She'll look at me in surprise. "It is? Gosh, I thought it was a lot earlier."

I refrain from reminding her that we have about 19 clocks in the house.

"Can I just finish this chapter?" she pleads.

"Sure," I say. Since she's reading a book I feel I can afford to be magnanimous.

Fifteen minutes later I go back to her room and ask her if she's finished the chapter.

"Oh, yeah. I just want to watch part of this show on TV. Please, Daddy? Please?"

"Absolutely not," I say in my stern father voice. "It's past time for bed."

Of course, it's another 15 minutes before she's actually in the bed what with pajamas and brushing teeth and other assorted stalling tactics that should, taking the parental view, have been completed much earlier in the evening.

I tell her good night and wearily head out of her room. I stop at her door and ponder the fact that tomorrow, as they say, is another day. Just like this one.

"Daddy?" my daughter calls out.

"What now?" I snap, unable to keep the irritation out of my voice.

"Love you."

I smile in the darkness. No argument here.

6 - Shop 'til You Drop

Going to the grocery store is an adventure when you have kids. Especially if they tag along.

My son ranks shopping at the grocery store somewhere between geometry tests and listening to his sister sing along to the latest hit song by the current hot pop group, despite the fact that he consumes the bulk of what goes into the grocery cart. So I happily allow him to beg off any such trips since the alternative is to drag down the aisles a grumbling kid with an attitude that would make a Hell's Angel blush and a mood so sour it could turn the grapes in the produce section to raisins.

My daughter, on the other hand, would shop for flip-flops in February. She considers it unhealthy, unnatural and probably illegal to leave a store without making a purchase. She gets upset if we go window-shopping and don't bring one home. So she eagerly volunteers to go along with me to the grocery store, visions of candy and sweets no doubt filling her head.

Which is one of the first things grocery stores hit you with as you walk in. We're in the store all of three seconds and she's already tugging at my sleeve, asking THE question: "Daddy, can I buy that, pulleeeeeze?"

"No," I respond sweetly but firmly, the very model of the patient and kindly father out on a shopping expedition with his loving and lovely daughter. "Let's see what else they might have," I suggest. "Besides, we need to get a cart."

"I'll do it," she says excitedly, racing over to the rows of carts. I smile at her youthful exuberance and how such simple things in life as selecting a transportation device can make kids happy.

I check my list only to be distracted by a loud clanking. It is, of course, my daughter, who is pushing a cart that issues a disturbing clang with each roll. It's also weaving precariously from side to side.

"Honey," I say, "I think we should try another cart. There's something wrong with that one."

"No, there's not," she replies defensively.

"Yes, there is," I counter patiently. "Look at the wheels. One of them isn't even moving. The other one is turned sideways."

"Daddy, it's the one I want. It'll work fine."

I sigh. I've learned that the trick with kids is not to try to win the battles, but the war. So I rarely even contest the skirmishes anymore. I settle for a gentle admonishment: "Be careful," I warn. "Don't run into anything. Or anybody."

We head out into the land of fruit and veggies. I'm pondering whether the objects under the sign that reads "plums" are really fruit or painted rocks when I hear a shriek. In a panic, I drop the purple object – part of my mind registers the opinion offered by my foot that the object definitely was of the mineral family – to see my daughter pointing at something while jumping up and down.

"Daddy! Blueberries! Can we get some? Huh? Pleeeze?"

"Why not?" I answer. She's grabbing boxes of berries, but I put only one in the cart, doing some quick calculations: Hmmm, that works out to about 42 cents per berry. Ah, well.

We push on. We argue briefly over whether we should buy a type of juice every drop of which she swears she will drink but which I know I will end up pouring down the sink. I distract her by pointing ahead to the seafood department.

Her eyes glowing, she stares at the lobsters patiently awaiting their fate in a bubbling tank.

"No," I say before she can even ask. I peruse the assortment of delectables from the sea.

"Daddy?"

"Yes, sweetie?"

"Can we get some shrimp?"

"Maybe. They sure look good, don't they?"

"Daddy?"

"Yes?"

"What does 'fresh frozen' mean?"

Good question. "It means they, um, froze the shrimp when they were, um, fresh."

"Oh." She digests this bit of fatherly wisdom. "Daddy?"

"Yes, what is it now?" I note that a tiny bit of exasperation has crept into my voice.

"So does that mean they freeze shrimp that aren't fresh?"

I consider this. "Well," I say, "I don't think I've ever heard of anyone selling rotten frozen shrimp, or putrid frozen shrimp – you know, the kind they had sitting out in the sun on the dock for a coupla days before they got around to throwing them on some ice - but I guess if they sell fresh frozen shrimp then somebody might. But don't worry, honey, they'd only sell that stuff in more sophisticated markets."

"Oh." That seemed to satisfy her. "Daddy?"

"What do you need now?" Yes, that definitely was a note of exasperation there.

"Can we get some crabmeat?"

"I dunno about that, baby. You have to be careful of what they call crab. Some of what passes for crabmeat never crawled around on the sea floor on legs. It's synthetic crabmeat."

"What's that mean?"

"It means they make it from reconstituted tree bark flavored with some of that not-so-fresh-frozen shrimp."

On we go. We spend 15 minutes debating the relative merits of the various types of cookies; I make a mental note to skip this aisle the next time we're here. The cart is clanking even louder now, and my daughter's steering is suffering because she's more interested in sightseeing than driving.

"Look out," I cry as she nearly smashes into a stacked display of cans. "Sorr-ee," she says haughtily, looking back at me as she runs into another shopper's cart. I apologize to the shopper and we move along. She's humming and I'm muttering.

"Stop here," I command her.

"Why?"

"Just do it."

"But this is just a bunch of medicines and stuff."

"Exactly. I need some aspirin. Here, the extra-strength, extra-jumbo size will do."

Finally, the end is in sight. "Honey," I say wearily, "could you get us a loaf of bread, please." I rub my head.

She throws a loaf in the crowded cart. "Careful," I say, "you don't want to squash it."

"Daddy?"

"Yes? What is it? What can I do for you?" Watch it, I tell myself. You're losing it.

"How come they sell bread in a bag?"

"What do you mean?"

"Well, they sell cookies in a box so they won't break. They sell crackers in a box. They sell beans in a can. Why do they sell bread in a bag? Why don't they sell it in a box so it won't get all smushed?"

Baffled, I ponder this.

"They don't sell eggs in a bag, do they?" she asks, and the thought makes her giggle. Even I manage a chuckle.

Another mystery of life left unsolved. I groan as we manhandle the cart up to the checkout line, where all sorts of buy-me attractions scream out to children.

"No, no, no, no, no," I say before she can get any words out of her mouth. Pouting, she heads over to inspect the machines that eat quarters.

I choose what I think is the line that will give us the shortest wait. After awhile, I notice that people who got in other lines after us are already leaving the store. I sigh. Up ahead I hear bits and pieces of an argument over why someone has to pay 89 cents for an item that was on sale last week for 79 cents.

At long last, my patience is rewarded. My groceries are scanned, the total is presented, the cashier calls my bank to confirm the loan, and we're outta there.

In the car, I fumble with my aspirin, muttering as I wrestle with the packaging. My daughter is singing. I'm gnawing at the aspirin bottle cap with my teeth. I finally toss it in the back seat in frustration.

"Honey, what person has done the most to change how we live in, oh, the last half of this century?" I ask my daughter.

She looks at me as though I've gone mad.

"Einstein, Edison…" I prompt.

"Daddy, what are you talking about?"

"None of the above," I continue. "My vote goes to the wacko who poisoned the Tylenol bottles a few years ago." My daughter has no clue as to what I'm talking about.

"You know, back in the old days, if you wanted a couple of aspirin, you simply unscrewed the bottle. No plastic seals. No childproof caps. No fancy packaging, putting bottles in boxes they ought to be using for bread. You didn't get a headache just trying to get into the things. Ah, life was so simple back then."

I look over at my daughter, who is looking at me in wonder. "Sorry, babe, I didn't mean to rant, there. It's just all that shopping kind of wore me out."

"That's OK," she assures me. She buckles up her seat belt. "Daddy?"

"Yes?"

"Can we go to the mall?"

7- The First Dance

I don't recall exactly when it was in my childhood that I discovered girls. But I do know that life hasn't been the same since.

Actually, I don't think I ever went through that standard grade-school phase when it was fashionable to detest classmates who happened to be representatives of the opposite sex; why, I even liked my sister. Most of the time. And I vividly remember sitting in Mrs. Westheimer's first-grade class scratching my head and thinking, as my friends debated the relative population densities of cooties on Mary Sue Cornbluth compared to Vicky Stinson, "Gee, I think they're both kind of cute."

Not so my son. How well I remember his cold stares in response to my parental advice in past years that he better be nice to the girls in his class, because one day he would want them to be nice to him. You would have thought I was predicting that one day he would request broccoli for supper.

How times change. At age 11, his grade-school years well behind him as he navigates the treacherous terrain of middle school, he is not the same person he was just a couple of years ago. He actually has opinions on the types of clothes he wears – and even stronger opinions on the types he won't. He eats more than does an adult. He's beginning to suspect that perhaps his father doesn't actually know everything there is to know in the world. He no longer is a pushover on the basketball court. He openly admits to liking girls. And now he is preparing to go to his first dance.

"Are you nervous, son?" I ask as he's getting ready.

"Why would I be nervous, Dad?" he responds, as though going to your first dance and making physical contact with girls in front of your peers is as routine as turning on the TV.

"Gosh, I don't know. I just remember that I was nervous when I went to my first dance." This, of course, is not exactly true. Petrified would be a more apt description.

"Well, I'm not."

"Good," I say, hastening to lie unconvincingly, "there's nothing to be nervous about, you know."

"I know, Dad."

I sigh. I realize he's about to that age when they know it all, or think they do. But then his mother appears in the room and quashes that notion.

"Is that what you're going to wear?" she asks sweetly.

"MOM!" Just like that, it's countdown, ignition, launch. Houston, we have gone ballistic.

"What's wrong with this?" he roars, suddenly near tears. "You don't ever like what I want to wear. Fine, I won't wear anything."

I bring up a mental picture of my son at the dance in his birthday suit and chuckle. I quickly wipe the smile off my face when I see them both glaring at me. Acknowledging that fashion is not my forte, I bow out of the action.

Apparently they reached some agreement on attire, for soon after they come down the stairs. I decide that no comment on the clothing selection is my safest course of action. Anyway, it's almost time to go – the moment of truth. I take a deep breath and call him over for a little private father-son chat.

"OK, here are a couple of things you need to remember," I begin. He looks at me as though I'm going to tell him water is wet. "Be polite. Don't be mean. Don't just hang out with the guys. Don't keep your hands in your pockets all night. Are you getting all this?" I add this last question because he's inspecting the ceiling.

"Sure, Dad," he responds casually.

"All right, then, you're set. You're not nervous, are you? Never mind." I scratch my chin. "But perhaps you better see if your mom has anything to add. You know, the girl's perspective."

They huddle up and whisper. I shake my head. For a family that doesn't keep secrets, I sure feel like I'm in the dark on a lot of things.

Off they go. The house is quiet. Very nice. I guess I need to get used to this; from here on out, he'll be going out more and more often. More dances, and then dates. Then he'll be wanting to borrow the car. Then he'll be out half the night. Then he'll hardly ever be around. I wonder how it's going. I hope it's not a disaster. I hope he's not a wallflower. I hope he has a good time. But maybe not too good a time.

Why is this so nerve-wracking, I ask myself. Get a grip. This is not that big of a deal, I tell myself. Then a chill goes down my spine. The big deal, I realize, will come in a few more years when my daughter is heading off to her first dance.

My wife returns. "Well, that's that," I say. "Do you think he'll be all right?" She assures me that he will be. "You know," I say, "it's hard to believe he's at a dance. With girls."

"I know," she says. "It's all happened so fast, hasn't it? Remember when we'd sit up in his room in a rocking chair, trying to get him to sleep when he was a baby?" She laughs at the thought. I fail to see the humor in the memory, and besides, something's in my eye. I blow my nose. "Yeah, those were some long nights. He sure was little, wasn't he? And he sure is big now."

She concurs with my penetrating insight, and adds, "He's growing up. You've got to let him do that, you know."

But nobody said it would be so hard.

Later, I go to pick him up at the dance. Loud noise is crashing out of the school cafeteria. "What's going on?" I shout at another parent standing outside waiting. "What's all that noise?"

"That's the music," she shouts back.

Oh. I knew that, as my kids would say.

Finally, the dance is over. My son emerges. "How'd it go?" I ask.

"Fine."

"Fine? Just fine?"

"Good."

"Good. Does that mean you had a good time? Did you dance with some girls?"

"Of course."

Of course. I sigh. Simple communication should not be this difficult. "So you had lots of fun?"

"Sure."

"More fun than, oh, say, playing basketball?"

He rolls his eyes and gives me one of those looks as if to say, "Gee, Dad, don't be such a doofus."

"Say, Dad," he says instead.

"Yes?"

"So can we play some basketball tomorrow?"

"Sure, son," I say. For some reason I have to clear my throat. "I don't see why not."

Whew. I haven't lost him yet.

8 - *Putting Away the Toys*

I played with dolls when I was a kid.

This was not something that I publicized as a boy, and for that matter it's not an easy admission to make as a man. The mitigating factor here is that my older sister threatened me with grievous bodily harm if I did not join her in the fun and fascinating world of Barbie. At least she let me play with the Ken doll.

I am reminded of this as I rummage in the attic for something or another and come across a large plastic container of my daughter's Barbie stuff. This, mind you, is merely her auxiliary Barbie supplies: the car, the camper, the Olympic gymnast outfit, the out-of-fashion friends. Her primary paraphernalia is still safely stashed somewhere in the nether regions of her closet, since on occasion she trots the dolls out and has them try on some of the 149 or so outfits they have accumulated over the years.

I am familiar with most of her Barbie stuff since as a dutiful dad I often joined her in the make-believe doll world when she was younger. If truth be known, my preferences for playtime with my children run toward activities that employ a ball. And while I personally find playing with miniature figurines tiresome - unless, of course, they are engaged in some military action or another - I feel obligated to spend at least a little time doing what my kids enjoy. Plus, I may as well put my experience with dolls to good use.

Anyway, my doll-playing days seem numbered, since my daughter, at age 9, would much rather dress herself up than her dolls. She is keenly attuned to current fashion and style, and willfully selects form over function at every turn:

"Dad, does this go together?" she will ask as she dresses for school.

"Um," I stall for time as I squint at her outfit. "Aren't those pants kind of short?"

"Daaaaddddy." She rolls her eyes. Where do they learn to do that, anyway? Is it part of the state-mandated curriculum in fourth grade: reading, long division, history, beginning eye-rolling and other expressions of impatience at the frankly unbelievably low level of intelligence in the parental units?

24

"They're supposed to be like that," she explains as if to a half-wit.

"Oh." I realize that my response could be interpreted as reinforcing her suspicions of paternal IQ levels. "Um, are those what they call pedal-pushers?"

There go the eyes again. I wince. "No, Daddy." She sighs. "They're called Capri pants."

"Oh." I focus on the rest of her attire. "Um, sweetie, don't you think it's a bit cold for that sleeveless top?"

"But it's always hot in school," she counters.

"But it's 12 degrees outside."

She ponders this bit of logic. Suddenly, tears well up in her eyes. Ah, I think, here we go again with some more of this ocular byplay.

"But this is what everyone is wearing," she sniffs.

"Are they wearing those kind of shoes, too?" I point at these clog-like things with heels. "How are you going to go to PE in those things?"

It's like well-drillers hitting a gusher. The tears stream down her face now. "You just don't want me to look nice. You just want me to look like a dork," she wails as she rushes back to her room.

Cowardice being the better part of valor - or something like that - I decide to call in the heavy artillery. "Honey," I call to my wife. "I need your help."

This overwhelming sense of fashion is not limited to clothing, either. My wife informs me that she has had a conversation with our daughter concerning leg shaving.

"Shaving whose legs?" I ask.

My wife rolls her eyes.

"Oh," I say. I frown. "Am I missing something? She doesn't have any hair on her legs yet."

"Apparently it's considered quite fashionable at that age."

"To shave their legs?"

"Yes."

"With a razor?"

"Well, duh."

"You learned that expression from her, didn't you?" I accuse. "And would people in this house stop doing that with their eyes? Why are they shaving their legs? I thought women hated doing that."

"We do. It just makes them feel grown up."

"I see," I say. I realize boys can't wait to shave. I couldn't when I was a kid. Of course, you don't realize that it's a procedure that loses its charm after, oh, about the third time you do it.

I don't know if girls ever get tired of makeup, though. My daughter already has more knowledge about makeup than I've accumulated in my lifetime, even though she's not allowed out of the house with any on. But of all the mysteries surrounding makeup, the biggest to me is when you're supposed to wear it.

Take, for instance, my daughter's initial Girl Scout camping trip. My wife, the troop leader, was discussing with the girls the types of things you need when camping.

"Makeup!" one of them said.

"CD players."

"Roller blades."

"Makeup."

They were distressed when informed that boom boxes would not be allowed on the camping trip, but they were downright distraught to learn that makeup kits were not a priority item.

"But our boyfriends might come by," one of them explained.

"Girls need to look nice," another said.

I can't help but ponder on the stereotypes being perpetuated here. What happened to the modern woman? But I realize that none of these young girls has ever actually been camping, so this will be an educational experience for them in more ways than one.

Gender stereotypes seem to be everywhere you look. Recently, while coaching my son's middle-school basketball team, we were taking a bus with the girls' team to a game at another school. The boys were being, well, stereotypical boys: stuffing their faces with every imaginable kind of junk food, genially harassing each other, and generally goofing around. The members of the girls' team were, well, putting on makeup.

At the time, I found those stereotypes depressing; we aren't as far along on the gender equality evolutionary ladder as we thought. But after giving it some thought I realize I was wrong. While the boys still treated the girls like boys have always treated girls, they took it in stride that girls could and should play basketball. The girls, on the other hand, had managed to combine

26

the best of both worlds: Not only were they going to play sports, but they were going to look like girls while they did it.

I was also struck by the sense of self-confidence these 12- and 13-year-olds seemed to project. A couple of the girls were trying to attract the attention of some of the boys, who were studiously ignoring them. Taking the rejection in stride, one of the girls, in a tellingly prescient warning, finally called out, "Just you wait until we're in high school. See if we give you the time of day."

I look at these girls and see my daughter in a few short years. I know my kids are changing, and I find myself struggling more and more to adapt to the changes. I find parenthood increasingly difficult the older our kids get.

Or perhaps it's all just more bewildering. I used to have all the answers when my kids asked me questions, but now I increasingly find myself deferring to my wife when it comes to matters of femininity. I feel out of my element, out of control. And worst of all I know the really tough times for my daughter - and me - are still to come.

I miss Barbie already.

Part II

The Nature of Things

9 – Getting To the Root of the Matter

Ah, spring. A time for renewal, for rebirth, for resurrection. In other words, time to put things in the dirt and watch them grow.

There's nothing quite like that sense of creation, of putting tiny seeds in the earth and waiting patiently for that first sign of life. For weeks and months fragile seedlings are carefully nurtured and worried over, until one proud day you realize they have become mature, responsible vegetation. And then, of course, you eat them.

Still, planning your outdoor plantings can be an adventure. Especially at my house, where there's nothing quite like a trip to the local garden shop in the spring to get the sap flowing.

The first rule is to act like you know what you're doing. This is difficult in my case, since I usually start out casually asking, "What type of cucumber plant is this?" and am politely told that it is, in fact, a cactus.

"I knew that," I say quickly. "Just checking to see if you did. So, where are the cukes? Ah, there they are. I believe I'll take this, um, bunch."

"Very good, sir. Are you full of manure?"

"I beg your pardon?"

"Manure, sir. Fertilizer. Your garden. Is it full of it?"

"Um, I don't believe it is."

"Well, you'll need at least half a ton, then. Are you acidic or alkaline?"

"Come again?"

"Your soil. Is it acidic or alkaline?"

I put on a thoughtful expression. "Well, now, I believe I have some of both."

"Both. Right. OK. Then you'll need some of this and some of that."

"This and that?"

"Right. Put this on the soil that is acidic to make it more alkaline, and put that on the soil that is alkaline to make it more acidic."

"Couldn't I just mix my dirt together. You know, commingle it?"

"Not if you want to achieve the proper balance in your soil."

"I'm still trying to achieve it in my life. What else?"

"Can I show you our latest irrigation system?"

"Irrigation?"

"Oh, yes. Vegetables like their water, you know. And you'll need a shovel, a spade, a pitchfork for the mulch ... Oh, dear, you do have mulch, don't you sir?"

"Mulch? Sure, sure. I mean, who doesn't have mulch, right? Say, how about some corn? There's nothing like good sweet corn, picked and shucked while the water's boiling."

"Right you are, sir. Here you go. And might I direct you to our hardware section?"

"Might you? Why?"

"For the fencing."

"Fencing? Am I going to keep cows now?"

"Raccoons."

"Raccoons? I'm going to raise raccoons?"

"Oh, no, sir. It's to keep them out. You'll need to erect a good, sturdy fence to keep those critters out. They love fresh corn, you know. And the little devils wait until the night before you pick it to eat it."

"They do?"

"Ah, they're crafty little devils, sir. And get a nice, strong combination lock for your gate."

"A combination lock? What, they can pick a regular padlock?"

"Absolutely. Of course, if you don't want to go the fence route, there are alternatives."

"Such as?"

"Television."

"A TV? You mean, put a TV out in my garden and the noise will scare them away?"

"Oh, no. But they love those infomercials and old movies that are on all night. They'll be so preoccupied, they'll forget about the sweet corn. Just make sure you don't grow any popcorn."

"Because they'll ... never mind. I don't want to know. But I don't think I want a TV blaring away in my garden all night. Any other options?"

"Of course. Let me give you the number of our private security force. For a rather reasonable fee, we can provide your garden with a highly trained, armed night security person."

"You mean have someone with a gun sitting in my garden all night ready to waste hungry wildlife? I don't think so. I'll take my chances on the fence."

"Very good, sir. Will that be electric or barbed wire?"

"Er, let's leave that issue unsettled for now, shall we? How about some of these tomato plants?"

"Excellent choice. Of course, you'll need stakes."

"I will?"

"Oh, yes, or they'll fall down. They need support. You can stake them or set them in these wire cages."

"And I'll be able to reach through the cage there to pick them?"

"Oh, you won't be picking them."

"I won't?"

"No, the blight will get them."

"The blight?"

"Oh, yes. Just before they're ready to be picked, they'll rot from the blight."

"Hmmm. Maybe I'll just plant some lettuce. You know, for a little salad."

"Rabbits."

"Rabbits? You mean..."

"'Fraid so. You'll need a fine wire mesh fence for them. String it right up along with your raccoon fence."

"What about sentry towers and search lights?"

"Ah, very good, sir. A sense of humor helps at times like these."

"I'm not so sure. So, how about something easy, like squash. Surely even a rank amateur gardener like me can grow a zucchini."

"No question. They'll grow almost anywhere. Here you go, and here's your computerized monitoring system."

"Monitoring system? What are you talking about?"

"Well, you have to keep an eye on your average zucchini. You check them in the morning, and think you can wait until that afternoon to pick them, and then you go back and the thing is as big as your house. This monitor is an early warning system; it beeps at the precise moment you need to pick the zucchini before it gets too big to handle."

"You're kidding me, right?"

"Oh, no, sir. Zucchini is not a laughing matter."

"Then why do I get the feeling the joke's on me? I'm starting to think I'll need a bank loan to finance this garden."

"Sir, what price can you put on natural, fresh, nutritious vegetables right out of the garden?"

I do some fast calculations in my head. "Off hand, I'd say about $14 per cucumber. I'm not sure I see the point in all this."

"The point, sir? Why, it's to reap the fruits of nature. And I might add, sir, that many people find gardening an excellent way to reduce stress."

"Are you mad? How in the world is this going to reduce stress? It's costing me a fortune to plant this garden. Then I'll slave away for weeks on end, all the while worrying that I'm spending all my quality time with eggplants instead of my kids, just so I can munch on some leaf that's probably got some creepy crawler on it."

"See there? I bet you've already forgotten all your other stressful troubles and problems, haven't you?"

"Hmmm. So, do you sell tractors?"

10 - Look, There's A Tree on My House

"Come quick, guys," my son announces breathlessly. "There's a tree about to fall!"

On my house.

Oh, the joys of home ownership. There's always some little job that needs doing. Painting the kids' bathroom. Waterproofing the deck. Cleaning out the gutters. Fixing a leaky faucet. Removing large trees from the roof.

Yes, these are the thrills apartment dwellers just can't buy. They must muddle on with such mundane tasks as unstopping a toilet, never knowing the larger pleasure of having a septic tank back up on them. And they miss out completely on the wonders of a flooded basement.

As a homeowner of some tenure, I figured I had experienced most of what there is to experience concerning home ownership, short of paying off a mortgage. The tree proved me wrong.

Exiting the house at my son's insistence, prepared to chastise him for whatever violence he had inflicted on some poor sapling sufficient to cause its imminent demise, I heard a sharp crack.

And another.

Instantly, putting to good use my expensive college education, I deduced that, as my son had surmised, a tree was about to fall.

And it wasn't a sapling, either.

"Run!" I croaked to the rest of my family, who had followed me out into the yard as I frantically looked about for which particular tree – I have many – had chosen this exciting moment to finally obey the law of gravity.

Alas and alack, it was not the 20-foot-tall dead pine down the driveway I had not yet had the time to chop down in the two years since its untimely demise. Nor was it one of those old apple trees grown crabby with age.

No, it was that 50-foot locust tree – yes, that's right, the one absolutely, positively   closest to the house – that had decided its time had come.

No wind was blowing, not a puff of breeze. But this magnificent arboreal specimen, which had snickered as Hurricane Hugo blasted past, which had barely blinked at the mighty Blizzard of '93, and which had laughed at many a blustery wind and howling storm since, uttered one last crack and toppled over.

Who knows how many trees fall unwatched – and, perhaps, soundlessly as philosophers would argue – in the forests of the world? This one, however, was viewed in stunned shock by my entire family, which had obeyed my warning to run away from the house a safe distance. My feet – not the brightest appendages of my body – had mysteriously not listened to my mouth. I hastily calculated the size of the tree and the distance I was from it and concluded, even though math is not one of my strongest subjects, that it was just possible that I was in big, leafy trouble, geometrically speaking.

Fortune smiled and I saw the tree was not going to fall on me.

It fell on my house.

It bounced slightly as we watched in awe, then settled with a sigh on the roof, branches artfully dangling down over the front door, the garage and the smashed gutter. Ha! I thought, I won't have to clean *you* out now.

Still, big trees don't fall on houses without making a little mess. The cleanup was, to say the least, extensive, although it did distract my wife, momentarily, from the ongoing wallpapering-the-bathroom project, now scheduled for completion well after retirement age.

The damage was added up: Broken rafters, shattered shingles, and a hole in the roof.

"It could be worse," my wife, ever the optimist, mused as we surveyed the damage.

"Look," I replied. "It's starting to rain."

For the next few days, a parade of interested parties dropped by. The tree cutters, to mutter, shake their heads, and give an estimate. The roofers, to mutter, shake their heads, and give an estimate. The insurance adjustor, to mutter, shake his head, and give us his card.

They all said the same thing: "Well, it's not too bad. You guys are lucky, really."

"Yeah," I mutter, "but not lucky enough for the tree to have fallen on *your* house."

We invited the tree to stay with us at our house for a couple of days. It was quite the talk of the neighborhood, although the busloads of tourists did start to tear up the yard, until the tree removal specialists arrived early one morning and detached it from the roof.

It turns out the tree had toppled due to forces of nature, meaning rot had gotten the better of it. I suppose it could happen to any of us and figured there was an important message there for us all to take to heart, such as live life to its fullest because you never know when a tree might fall on you.

So, dear, you can just forget about that little basement-cleaning project.

11 - *Making a Mountain Out Of a Mole Hill*

"Hello, Department of Agriculture. How may I help you?"

"Um, yes, hello. I've got a problem, and I was hoping you could help me."

"Certainly, sir. Do you need us to subsidize a crop nobody wants to buy or have us pay you not to grow a crop somebody does want?"

"Um, neither. I was hoping you could help me with a pest control problem."

"Oh, my, yes. What sort of pest, sir? Fruit flies? Slugs? Japanese beetles? Political commentators?"

"Moles, actually."

"Moles? Oh, well then, sir, I'll refer you to the CIA."

"No, no, not that kind of moles. The ones that burrow underground. They've made a mess of my yard. There are mounds of dirt all over the yard, and the little buggers have tunneled all over the place. It looks like a moonscape out there."

"And you think this could be caused by moles?"

"Well, yeah. They do this to my yard every year. I'm sick and tired of it. I've tried different things to get rid of them, but nothing seems to work."

"Such as?"

"Well, one year I tried these windmill devices. You stuck this pole in the ground with a small windmill on top, and it would cause the pole to vibrate and scare off the moles."

"How interesting."

"Yeah, and I thought it was working for awhile, too, but then I realized that the little critters has simply wired up tiny generators to the windmills and were using them to power their little televisions and refrigerators and stuff, so they just weren't out there digging as many tunnels."

"Really?"

"Then I tried gum."

"Gum? You chew gum to get rid of moles? How fascinating."

"No, no, no. You stick gum down the mole holes. They prefer Juicy Fruit."

"Sir, there are laws against making crank calls to your government..."

"No, listen, I'm serious. They eat the gum but supposedly they can't swallow it and choke on it."

"How sadistic. I'll pretend I didn't hear that part of the conversation or else I fear I would be forced to report you to the ASPCA for cruelty to animals."

"Cruelty to animals? But these are moles. You know, little blind mice."

"You're not chopping off their tails, too, are you?"

"Of course not. But they're still here despite the gum. In fact, every time I walk around my yard I go crazy listening to the muffled sounds of dozens of little mouths snapping their gum. So I was wondering if I could try something different. I was wondering if I could borrow some of the DEA's confiscated crack cocaine or something and slip it down one of the mole tunnels."

"Why on earth would you do that?"

"So that a whole generation of moles gets hooked on illegal narcotics and loses interest in becoming constructive members of mole society. Who knows? Before long, there could be gangs of punk moles roaming underground, spray painting tunnel walls, staking out the territory, battling each other with little Uzis blazing away in their tiny claws. They won't have any time for more digging."

"Sir, speaking of illegal narcotics…"

"Hey, I'm desperate here. What can I do?"

"Have you tried peaceful coexistence?"

"What are you, the State Department?"

"Just a thought, sir. Hmmm. I know; you could start a ranch."

"A ranch? What kind of a ranch? Oh, no, you don't mean…"

"A mole ranch. Sure. And your government would gladly let you have access to vast acres of national grazing lands at a nominal cost to assist you in your ranching."

"You mean you guys provide welfare for ranchers?"

"Oh, no, sir. Not welfare. It's agricultural assistance."

"Excuse me, but how the heck am I going to run a mole ranch? I mean, what do I have to do, hire a bunch of moleboys to ride around on little miniature ponies with tiny string lassos to herd them? And I don't even want to think about branding their little butts. The moles, I mean."

"You're right, sir, that does not conjure up a pretty picture."

"Nor is the sight of whole herds of moles roaming the range. I want to get rid of them, not get more."

"So you're saying you don't want our free brochure 'The Joys of Subsidized Ranching?' If you act now, we'll throw in, absolutely free, our exciting video 'Exotic Breeding Techniques for Fun and Profit.' "

"Um, I believe I'll pass. So can you just recommend a pesticide or something that will get rid of them?"

"Oh, no, sir. I couldn't do that. Moles are a protected species. You can't use poison on them."

"I can't? Then what can I do?"

"Well, trapping is allowed."

"Trapping? Why would I want to trap them?"

"For humane reasons, of course, sir. And then they could be relocated."

"You want me to trap a bunch of moles and relocate them? Where would I take them? And who would want them?"

"Well, you could take them out and free them in the wild."

"But I live out in the wild."

"Well, then, sir, you wouldn't have far to go, then would you?"

"How about I stick a hose down one of the holes and flood them out?"

"Oh, I wouldn't do that, sir."

"You wouldn't?"

"Oh, no, sir. Once you've flooded your property we would have to declare it wetlands. Then all the species on your property would be protected."

"All the species?"

"Absolutely. Such as your mice, your mosquitoes, your flies, your snakes, your…"

"I get the picture."

"Plus, if your property is a wetlands, there would be a prohibition on any sort of improvements. It would be environmentally protected against development."

"Are you serious?"

"Oh, yes, sir. In fact, you wouldn't even be able to sell your property, unless of course you sold it to a developer who wanted to put a shopping center there."

"A shopping center?"

"Or a mall. Those are the only things the government allows wetlands to be converted into."

"I should have known. So what you're saying is I'm stuck with these moles?"

"Oh, no, sir. I'm sure if you talk to the Pentagon they would gladly use your yard as a practice bombing range. They're fairly precise, you know, what with those smart bombs and all."

"I don't think so. So what you're basically telling me is that I'm going to have to live with them?"

"We seem to be running out of options, sir."

"Hmmm. Well, I guess there's only one thing to do."

"And that is, sir?"

"Adopt 'em."

"You're going to adopt your moles?"

"Sure. That way I can declare them as dependents. Get some tax benefits out of them with the IRS."

"I'm not sure that will work, sir."

"Hey, you don't know my accountant."

12 - Stormy Weather

For some reason, summer brings out something fanciful in meteorologists, a rather sedate crew not normally given over to whimsical behavior. But the thought of stormy weather must cause some sort of low pressure system around the upper cranial region, because every year with the onset of hurricane season they feel compelled to trot out a whole list of names for these once and future storms.

Personalizing ferocious ocean storms is rather a quaint tradition, although one probably underappreciated by the owner of some luxurious seaside home that has been reduced to three pilings in the sand after being visited by, say, "Otto." And, to their credit, the official hurricane-namers years ago dropped the sexist practice of using only female names for these wild and windy visitors.

Of course, meteorologists' imaginations only go so far; the World Meteorological Organization, which comes up with the names, actually only has six lists of names that are used in shifts. So the names of hurricanes used this year were used a half-dozen years ago, and will be used again in a few years. If a hurricane is a memorable one, its name is retired.

My question is if hurricanes are going to be given names, why on earth do they get the ones they have? What's with, for instance, Danielle, Odette, Gaston and Philippe? Are these storms planning to emigrate from France? Don't they have the decency to Americanize their names if they're going to come all the way across the Atlantic just to wreak havoc on some poor, innocent beach resort?

Another thing: What happened to the names beginning with Q, U, X, Y and Z? Their omission is tantamount to discrimination of the first rank, an odious enough practice for a government but simply shocking in an agency residing in the scientific community. Can these scientific minds not come up with Quincy, Ulysses, Xavier, Yolanda or Zeus if they're going to use Ophelia, Chantal, and Humberto?

And what's up with the weird spellings of names such as Shary and Hermine and Virginie? Are these scientists illiterate or are they simply trying to pull a few fast ones, kind of a pop quiz on a public that dozes off during the lectures about getting the heck out of the way of hurricanes before they hit?

Hurricanes, by the way, are interesting meteorological phenomena, and many people are fascinated with the storms whether or not they're on a first-name basis with them. They like to observe these huge storms up close and personal even after being advised to relocate elsewhere; these people are known in meteorological circles by their scientific name: idiots.

Anyway, it would seem that the people in charge of the hurricane naming process are not taking their jobs all that seriously – a dangerous attitude when dealing with nature. After all, hurricanes such as Wilfred, Fabian, Paloma and Sebastien might think they're being made fun of – "Yo, Fabian, let's see what you got, big boy. You call *that* wind?" Next thing you know they're retiring a name because Stan was trying to impress Vicky.

Perhaps the naming process should be contracted out. Let someone else have a shot at it and see it we can't come up with designations that have a bit more, well, pizzazz. Let's face it: It's hard to think about running from Dolly, or boarding up your windows for Larry, or being intimidated by Nana. But Screamin' Banshee or Sand Blaster or even Thor do the trick.

Or we could let the people who come up with car names take on the job. They could name storms Thunderbird, Mustang, Blazer, or Tornado.

And why is it that hurricanes and cyclones are the only storms that get names? Why not name other meteorological events? Certainly there could be a thunderstorm Teddy or a hailstorm Hannah or a blizzard Beulah.

Why stop there? Let's have a rainy day Ralph. Let's have the weather forecaster announce that, tomorrow, showers Phil and Nancy are expected in the afternoon. And in the early morning, fog – today called Horace – will be in evidence. For the weekend, plenty of sunshine is expected: Saturday, sunny day Fred will arrive, with partly cloudy sky Agnes making an appearance on Sunday.

Whatever the weather is, it ought to be called by a name. This will make weather much more personal for all of us, and perhaps give us a bit more insight into the mysteries of meteorology.

And to be on the safe side, always take your umbrella with you. Especially if they're calling for Ralph.

13 - *Trimming the Tree and All That Jazz*

The holidays used to be a wondrous, magical time - back when the kids were innocent little tykes who earnestly believed everything their parents told them, such as how Santa Claus would find a way in even though your house didn't have a chimney, you better be good or you wouldn't get any presents, and broccoli is an acquired taste.

Nowadays, though, as the kids grow older and wise up while the parents just get older and more wizened, it seems the tinsel has lost a bit of its luster. Around our house, the turning of the calendar page used to be accompanied by cries of delight: "It's Christmas time again!" Lately, it's coming out more like "It's Christmas time *again*?"

Commercialization no doubt is to blame for much of the blasé attitude; after all, it's hard to get but so excited about a holiday that starts as soon as the witches' costumes go on sale and you begin to be bombarded with incessant inducements to single-handedly spend the republic out of its economic doldrums by purchasing overpriced merchandise to give to people you haven't given a second thought to for the past year who don't need any more stuff anyway and will probably return it for something else just as soon as the post-holiday sales gear up.

The commercialization has even filtered down to Christmas trees, which is a pretty big industry where I live. It's a credit to the craftiness of the mountain people that they can get their supposedly more sophisticated neighbors down in the flatlands to shell out the equivalent of a week's worth of groceries for, let's face it, a piece of vegetation that is most emphatically living impaired.

But trees are one of the most beloved of holiday symbols, and the whole tree selection process is what usually gets the sap rising, so to speak, for the holiday fun ahead. In my family we all pile in the car and head off to the Christmas tree lot so that everyone can have a say in picking out the absolutely perfect specimen, which would metamorphose on the roof of the car on the ride home into a crooked, broken-branched pine that had mysteriously sprouted two trunks, some sort of alien-looking fungus on the bark and which required a chain saw to hack off the three feet of height needed to cram it in under the ceiling.

It is the father's job, naturally, to string the lights on the tree, this being the technical aspect of the project and requiring great expertise in matters of a, well, technical nature, not to mention extensive experience in being mildly electrocuted by faulty wiring. It is the wife's job to survey the light-stringing with a critical eye and pronounce that, yes, there are some blank spots on the tree and is that all the lights that are going to be put on the tree?

Over the years, I have accumulated enough strings of lights to decorate a middle-aged sequoia, so this year to forestall any criticism of shortlightedness I wrapped the tree up like a mummy, winding string after string of lights around and around. After inviting spousal perusal, my wife squinted, frowned and said it looked OK.

"OK?" I said. "Just OK?"

"It's ... fine," she amended.

"Fine?" I echoed, hearing the damning phrase of mediocrity. "What's wrong with it?"

"Nothing ... really. It's fine. Really."

"So what are you saying? Really."

"Nothing. It's just that, well, a picky person might say that there was kind of a hole right there."

"Right where?" I demand. "There? There's not a branch there," I declare smugly. "You can't have lights where there isn't a branch." This is the kind of highly advanced technical expertise concerning light stringing of which mere ornament-hangers and tinsel-throwers don't have a clue about.

"How about this?" she asks sweetly, rearranging my carefully placed lights to fill the hole.

"How about we break out the eggnog?" I say.

Once the lights are on the tree, the hard-core decorating commences. Musty boxes are dragged out of the attic, each containing its own treasure trove of ornaments – most of them inexpensive, glittery gewgaws that are priceless in their sentimentality. These fragile balls and bells and snowflakes and candy canes and assorted members of the animal kingdom are what help make the whole tree experience so special. The ornaments carry the traditions of Christmas on from year to year, bringing forth memories of happy holidays gone by.

"All right, kids, c'mon and let's decorate the tree," I call out.

"Now?" they exclaim.

"What do you mean, 'now?' Of course, now."

"But, Dad, I'm in the middle of this video game," my teen-age son points out.

"And my favorite TV show is coming on," my younger daughter yells down from her room.

I frown at my wife. "Remember," I say, "when they would come in screaming with excitement to decorate the tree? Now they're screaming from their rooms to be left alone."

I shake my head. "Kids!" I holler up the steps. "C'mon. It'll be fun. We'll play some Christmas music and get out all the neat stuff for the tree." To my wife I say, "Maybe we'll need a touch more of that eggnog."

The kids come dragging down the steps, faces long and eyes rolling. "So, Dad, where are the decorations?" my son asks.

I consider this. "Well," I say, scratching my head, "Perhaps we could try these boxes scattered around the living room."

They rummage in the boxes and desultorily begin to hang ornaments on the tree. My wife and I watch with satisfaction for a moment and then we join in, humming along to "Deck the Halls."

"Um, son," I say after a while. "That's probably enough of those red balls, don't you think?"

"Why?" he enquires.

"Well, you've got about 12 of them all hanging on three branches all together. Don't you think you could spread them around a little?"

"Gee, Dad, you said you wanted us to help you decorate the tree. If you don't like how I do it..."

"No, no," I say hastily. "Here, why don't you start in with this box?" I sigh and notice that my daughter is bending a branch to the breaking point with a heavy glass ornament.

"Sweetie, that's not going to work," I tell her.

Tears form in her eyes. "Well, how was I supposed to know that!" she wails. "I'm trying my best to do this, you know! You don't have to yell at me!"

"I'm not yelling," I say, my voice rising. "And you're doing just fine. It's just that ornament is too heavy ... now what?" The kids are pushing and shoving.

"She grabbed the ornament I was going to hang," my son informs me.

"Well, he took the one I wanted," she fires back.

"Did not."

"Did, too."

"Enough!" I shout. "Can somebody turn that *&#$ music down? I can't hear myself think in here. Sheesh, guys, c'mon, it's Christmas. Can't we all just get along?"

They glare at each other, arms crossed.

"Honey," I say to my wife. "Maybe I'll take a tad bit more of that eggnog. And you can leave off the egg."

I flop down on the couch. "You know, guys," I say, "We don't have to do this."

"Fine," they humph.

"We don't have to have a tree."

"Great."

"We don't have to celebrate Christmas."

"So what?"

"We don't have to have any presents."

They look at each other. They grab some ornaments.

"You know, Christmas is about more than trees and ornaments and presents," I tell them. "It's about peace and love and joy to the world."

"We know, Dad," they say. "We're sorry."

"Good," I reply. "Your mom and I are going to sit on the couch for a bit and enjoy some good cheer. You guys work on the tree for awhile."

"Sure, Dad," they chorus.

"And when you get done," I add, "you can start on the outdoor lights."

14 - There's Something about Snow

Snow.

There's something magical and mystical about that white stuff. Unlike its first cousin in the precipitation family, rain, snow always comes as a surprise, and is never taken for granted.

It also does weird things to people. My theory is that snow somehow short-circuits the Earth's electro-magnetic field, thereby altering human brain waves. How else to explain people's flaky behavior when the snow falls?

Consider the simple act of driving a car. Snow profoundly affects not only the mechanics of driving but the operation of automobiles as well.

Some drivers take all the precautions they can think up, putting chains on the studded snow tires of their four-wheel drive sport utility vehicles, then loading them down with all the recommended paraphernalia of winter driving: bags of salt and sand, a snow shovel, a traction mat, ice scrapers in assorted sizes, jumper cables, a tow chain, blankets, flares, flashlights, portable gas grills, you name it. Lighter loads have been taken to conquer Everest.

Other drivers assume that their automobiles, which after all cost them more than the average lifetime income of all but 13 nations of the world, will carry them to their destinations no matter what the climatological conditions. These are the people with a blind faith in technology: The ones you see blithely cruising along ice-covered roads at 65 miles per hour in their Buicks with bald tires, and the ones to whom you later wave as you drive by the tow truck hauling their car out of the ditch.

You do not feel too sorry for them, either, because you hope that they spent their time in the ditch wisely, perhaps becoming more intimately acquainted with all the working parts of their automobile, such as the turn signal.

Sometimes people have appropriate cars for winter driving, but refuse to prepare them for actual use. We all have seen these people motoring down the road with their faces all scrunched up and peering out a tiny hole they've hacked through the ice crusting their windshields, with about two feet of snow still packed onto the car's roof like some sort of arctic luggage rack.

When they're not engaged in trying to transport themselves in the snow, people are busy making their personal winter fashion statement. Some use the weather as an excuse to dress down, shedding that coat and tie for jeans and a flannel shirt at the first sign of a flurry, or losing the dress and heels for sweat pants and a pair of boots a lumberjack would be proud of if even a shred of ice is rumored to remain in the parking lot.

At least they're going with function over style. There are plenty of people who spend hundreds and thousands of dollars on glow-in-the-dark attire made with space-age materials designed to keep the wearer warm, dry and on the cutting edge of fashion – even when they're sitting on their butts on the sidewalk.

It's always a good idea, of course, to wear plenty of layers of clothes in cold weather, but even this can be overdone. Some people get so bundled up they can barely move, so if they fall down all they can do is lie on their backs feebly waving their arms and legs in the air like an overturned beetle.

Snow also seems to have a strange affect on people's gastronomical inclinations. The first flake hasn't even hit the ground before lines form in the grocery stores, everyone clutching two or three gallons of milk and half a dozen loaves of bread as though all the cows on the planet had suddenly died right after eating all the wheat in the world. It doesn't seem to matter that these same people will be driving by the same grocery store tomorrow; panic grips them as they fear they may be holed up for the entire winter with nothing to put in their cereal and nothing with which to make a sandwich.

Snow can make people do things they normally wouldn't dream of doing. Couch potatoes who wouldn't get up to turn the channel on their TV will trudge up a hill for a half mile just to whiz down a hill on a sled. Serious sorts who haven't laughed in years suddenly are acting like kids, flinging balls of snow at one another. Or they start eyeing the dog to see how it would measure up attached to one end of a rope with a sled at the other.

And snow sometimes makes otherwise honest people depart from the path of truth. They'll get to work only to immediately engage in a meteorological pissing contest, scoffing at the thin layer of snow outside the office, and sneering at co-workers' tales of digging out at home. "That's nothing," they'll announce smugly, "there was at least half a foot more at my house, and the temperature was 10 degrees colder to boot."

Why having a house situated on the one lot in the county with the absolutely worst weather in the state would be a source of pride is a mystery to me.

It's a natural seasonal pastime for mountain residents to either brag outrageously or complain vehemently about the weather, unless you are talking to a flatlander, in which case custom demands that you be nonchalant about it. No matter that you threatened that very morning to pack the family off to the Bahamas if you saw one more flake of that damn white stuff; when conversing with an out-of-towner you merely yawn and remark about how this latest snow isn't anything, certainly nothing to compare to the one back in '94, or was it '88, when you had to tunnel out the upstairs window just to let the dog out.

Still, even if it does make people slightly daffy, snow is wondrous and special, a dazzling testament to nature's diversity and mystery.

Of course, spring ain't too shabby, either.

15 -The Nature of Things to Come

"Hello there, sir. I'd like to speak to the head of the household, please."

"She's not here right now. Perhaps I can help you."

"Ah, it's the other way around. I'm calling today to help you. You see, I'm a representative of Virtual Nature, Inc."

"Excuse me?"

"Virtual Nature. We're a relatively new company on the cutting edge in the manufacture of synthetic representational models of organic arboreal specimens."

"Say what?"

"Synthetic representational..."

"No, no, no. You're going to have to say it in a language other than Sales-Speak."

"We sell alternatives to trees."

"Alternatives to trees? Why on earth would you want to do that?"

"Why, sir, don't you keep up with current events? Do you not follow the news? The real things are downright dangerous."

"What things? Trees? They're dangerous?"

"Absolutely, sir. Haven't you heard about all the forest fires in the past several months?"

"Well, yeah, but..."

"But nothing. Homes have been destroyed, personal property damaged. Whole towns have been threatened. Not to mention shopping malls."

"Yes, and your point is?"

"Why, the federal government has determined that trees are so dangerous that the White House has proposed that the national forests be turned over to the logging industry. Strictly for our protection, of course."

"Is this some sort of crank call? Because..."

"Oh, no, sir, I assure you I'm for real. Honest, could I make this up? The government feels that only the logging industry can adequately manage fuel reduction in the forests."

"Fuel reduction?"

"Sure. You know, anything that will burn."

"You're telling me that the government wants to cut down all its trees to prevent forest fires?"

"Pretty nifty idea, huh?"

"What's next? Is the government going to kill all the bald eagles so they won't be on the endangered species list any longer?"

"You know, you might be on to something there. I wonder if they've thought of that?"

"I find it pretty hard to believe that the government would do something like this. I mean, these are our national forests we're talking about."

"Oh, it's not just the national forests that concern the government. They see every tree as pretty much a fire waiting to happen. There's a pretty extensive government campaign to protect the American public from this insidious danger that lives among us. I mean, if you think about it, it's downright frightening: Trees are everywhere."

"We can only hope."

"The government's next step is public involvement in fire prevention. I understand there will be some tax breaks for chain saw purchases. And have you seen the new Smokey the Bear campaign? The one where he's got the ax and says, 'Only you can prevent forest fires: Clear-cut some woods today.' "

"That's sacrilege!"

"Nah, it's just marketing. Anyway, that's where we come in. We foresee a huge market now for synthetic alternatives to nature."

"Synthetic alternatives?"

"Yes. You know, trees."

"I think you've been out in the sun too long. So you're selling plastic trees?"

"Well, actually it's more of a polyurethane blend. Initial tests show that they are very durable. They'll last at least as long as your average real tree. Of course, we're not talking 500-year-old sequoia here."

"Of course. Let me ask you something. Do you really think anyone is going to buy your, er, product?"

"But of course. Why, we already have a huge government contract; they have whole forests to replace, after all."

"With plastic trees. I don't believe it. What happens when the wind blows?"

"Ah. Excellent question. All of our trees are built to withstand gusts of up to gale force. You see, they come with tie-down anchors. Sort of like tent stakes. We call them 'root stakes.'"

"Is that right?"

"Although the 50-foot models require cement root stakes. If you bury them 10 feet down we guarantee they'll withstand a hurricane. Category 1 only, of course."

"I don't see how you could be any fairer."

"We're offering a special right now; buy two 50-foot models, and you get your choice of a sapling for free."

"And just what kind of, um, trees would these be?"

"All our models come with real imitation wood-grain trunks in your choice of colors: oak, cherry, maple, pine or mahogany. To be honest, the mahogany's a bit on the high end, though."

"I'll bet."

"They come in deciduous and evergreen models, as well. With the evergreens, you can get a pine scent sprayed on for a very reasonable extra cost."

"What do the deciduous ones come with? Plastic squirrels and rubber nuts?"

"Hah, hah. Very good, sir. A sense of humor is so valuable in these troubled times."

"I think so."

"Seriously, though, the squirrel idea is not too bad. I'll just jot down a note here for research and development…"

"Hey, happy to help."

"Now then, where were we? Oh, yes. Deciduous models. They come with your choice of leaves."

"Leaves?"

"Detachable."

"Detachable?"

"Sir, do you hear an echo on this line? Never mind. Yes. The deciduous models all come with detachable leaves."

"Let me get this straight. You actually sell fake trees with fake leaves that fall off?"

"Isn't it wonderful what they're doing with modern science and technology? But, please, we prefer the term 'inorganic' to 'fake.' The detachable-leaf models are for those homeowners who want to continue to experience the nostalgic autumn ritual of high-decibel leaf-blowing."

"You're kidding, right?"

"Not at all. Although we do caution against jumping into a pile of our leaves. They're quite a bit more, um, durable than the natural variety."

"I can see where it wouldn't quite be the same thing,"

"They can be reattached, naturally, so you can have leaves on your trees winter, spring, summer or fall."

"I don't know. All that shade might kill my grass."

"Ah, not to worry."

"Don't tell me…"

"Oh, yes, indeed. We have a full line of authentic artificial lawns…"

16 - When It Rains It Pours

"We now take you to our special liquid precipitation specialist, Al Wette. Al, what do you have for us here at the Climate Channel?"

"Rain, Peter. I have rain here in Seattle."

"Wow! Rain? You don't say."

"I do say, Peter. We have a torrential sprinkling right now, but we could see it change anytime to a heavier light shower. This is, indeed, one of the worst light rains they've seen in the Pacific Northwest in several days."

"Al, what about flooding?"

"That's a very good question, Peter. Right now, we're looking at only minor puddling, but the streets are already wet, so they're slippery. Drivers should take precautions and use their windshield wipers. As far as major flooding, I'd say we could be in for some if it keeps raining for, oh, say another 40 days. And nights."

"OK, well, thanks for that report, Al. Next, we take you to Phoenix and our solar heat expert, Summer Farr. Summer?"

"Thanks, Pete. Well, the weather here is extremely extreme. We've got temperatures in the 90s, so it's brutal. But the real problem is the sun."

"Why's that, Summer?"

"It's shining, Pete. It's relentless. There are no clouds in the sky whatsoever. The sun is just sitting up there scorching everything. I have to say, Pete, that it's like a desert here in Phoenix."

"Wow! Very vividly put, Summer. How are the citizens holding up in that heat wave?"

"Pretty well, so far. They're all inside in the air conditioning. You don't want to be out in this sun without a hat and sunscreen, Pete, I can tell you that. And the glare from that constant sun could make driving hazardous, so motorists are being encouraged to take precautions and wear sunglasses."

"All righty, then, Summer, thanks for that report. We're going now to the nation's Midwest, where correspondent 'Pecos' Bill Jones is standing by. Bill?"

"Thanks, Peter. I'm standing here in a mobile home park in Plainview, Kansas, where a killer tornado is expected."

"Wow! Bill, can they track those things that accurately now?"

"Well, no, Peter, but everyone knows mobile homes attract twisters like flies to, um, cow pies. So it's just a matter of time before one hits."

"I see. And how long have you been waiting?"

"Six weeks. But..."

"Hmm. Bill, perhaps we could find you another assignment."

"No, no, that's all right, Peter. I'm sure a tornado will be along any time now. Those babies can pop up in a second. And when one does, we'll be right here ready for it."

"OK, Bill, whatever you say. Thanks for that report. Let's go quickly now to our special coastal correspondent, Sandy Dunn, at the beach, where I understand he has a late-breaking weather report."

"That's right, Peter. I'm standing here on the beach in Florida. There are waves breaking behind me – huge three- and four-foot monsters just crashing into the sand – and we have a pretty stiff mild breeze blowing off the ocean. I've never seen anything like it; of course, this is the first time I've been to the beach."

"Wow! So is there a hurricane approaching?"

"Not right now, Peter, but we have reports from the National Dangerous Weather Administration that one could hit this area."

"How soon would that be, Bill?"

"Well, during hurricane season, but that's only a few very short months away."

"I see."

"Still, it's blowing pretty good here, Peter. The wind is blowing sand around and there's a lot of salt in the air. Picnicking conditions are not great because of the danger of sand in your sandwiches."

"I could see where that could be a real problem."

"Yes, and driving conditions here on the beach are not good. Authorities are warning motorists to stay off the beach because of the deep sand and the tide moving in. Only emergency vehicles are allowed on the beach at this time, we are told."

"Any other problems there on the beach, Sandy?"

"We've had reports, so far unconfirmed, that just south of our location that at least two people and as many as five, and again this is all unconfirmed rampant speculation, have been hit by seagulls."

"You mean the birds just flew into them?"

"Um, no, not exactly, Peter. They, er, flew over them and, um…"

"Ah, I think we get the picture, Sandy, and not a pretty one at that. Thanks for that report. We have an update from Texas, now, with reporter Rock Fallon. Rock?"

"Yes, Peter, I'm looking out at a violent, destructive and, some might say, life-threatening hail storm. Ow! It's incredible. Ouch! We've got hailstones the size of, oh, basketballs coming down."

"Basketballs?"

"OK, maybe softballs. Ow! Or baseballs. Maybe ping-pong balls. Ouch! Or marbles. Peas, perhaps. Young peas. Ouch!"

"Rock, they appear to be hitting you."

"Yes, Peter. Ouch! Ow! They are."

"Why don't you go inside?"

"Peter, I'm a weather reporter. The weather is – ow! – outside. Besides, I wanted to wear – ow, that one hurt – my snazzy new all-weather gear."

"Right. Let's go live now to the mountains of North Carolina where I understand a severe winter storm is brewing. Let's go to our severe winter storm expert, Wendy Hill."

"Thanks, Peter. Yes, people here are hunkering down for what could be the worst winter storm of the winter, if not the last several winters. In fact, some people could say that this might be the worst winter storm of the past millennium, if not the past several millennia…"

"Um, Wendy, what is it doing there exactly?"

"Snowing, Peter. It's snowing up a storm. This is officially at least a full gallon and two-loaf storm."

"A gallon and what?"

"A full gallon of milk and two loaves of bread, Peter. It's how we measure the severity of winter storms. It's based on how much of the basics you stock up on at the grocery store. Snow flurries are just a pint and a slice; snow showers are a quart and half-a-loaf …"

"How fascinating. So this is a big one, then?"

"I should say so, Peter. We have near-blizzard conditions."

"Near-blizzard conditions. Does that mean a blizzard is nearby or that the existing conditions are similar to a blizzard?"

"It means we've got heavy snowfall in the air with slight meltage on the ground."

"And this means...?"

"This means we could start seeing accumulations soon."

"So there's no actual snow on the ground yet?"

"Not heavy accumulations. Flakes are definitely landing, but are melting when they hit. But it could start piling up at any minute and when it does we could get several inches. Or feet. Maybe several feet. And ice. We could get ice and sleet. Freezing rain, too. That would mean icy conditions, Peter. People are being warned to stay off the roads in case snow, ice, sleet or freezing rain falls. They're urged to stay in their homes and turn the heat on, because it's freezing out here. Unless the power goes off, in which case they should get in their cars and go someplace warm. Like Florida."

"I don't know about that, Wendy. We're getting reports of mild breezes and heavy humidity down there."

"Well, then, Peter, I'm not sure any place on Earth is safe from the weather."

"Thank you for that ominous report, Wendy. That's right, folks, the entire planet could be in peril from our predictions of extreme weather conditions. And now, don't go away; right after these messages we'll have a special report on "Fiendish Fog: The Dangers Within.""

Part III

Learning Life's Lessons

17 - Lessons Of Life Are Bittersweet

What a lesson money can teach. Especially if you're 6 years old.

Since it is the duty and responsibility of parents to ensure that their children learn about life, my son's stated interest in what would be his inaugural business enterprise was warmly supported.

A lemonade stand? What a tremendous idea. Not particularly innovative by modern industrial or technological standards, but a proven winner.

So the venture took shape. He drew up the sign. We haggled over the pricing. He helped make the lemonade, and the brownies that were going to help pad the bottom line.

The big day arrived. He set up shop outside his mother's office. Sidewalk traffic was brisk. Business boomed. An entrepreneur was born as my shy son was transformed into a charming salesman with a magnetic personality – all through the magical allure of cold, hard cash.

At last the long business day ended. The lemonade container was dry. The brownies were history. The till was full.

The accounting was at hand. Slowly, he counts the bills and the change.

"How much, son?" I ask.

"Twenty bucks and two cents," he answers with pride.

TWENTY BUCKS! Who would have thought this venture would have been so lucrative? I congratulate him, my mind scheming with thoughts of franchising the operation. If a kid can make $20 in a shoestring operation, what might a college-educated adult do with this concept?

Visions of becoming the Lemonade King or the Baron of Brownies flit through my head. A fortune to be made…

A sudden thought intrudes.

"What's with the two cents?" I ask.

My son gives the standard kid response to practically any question of significance.

"I dunno."

"Someone gave you two cents?"

"I guess."

"As a tip or something?"

He gives this question considered thought. "I dunno," he says at last.

Unquestionably, this is executive material in the making. But visions of fiscal grandeur give way to pangs of parental responsibility.

"Well, son," I say, "I guess you've learned the value of money today, right?"

"You bet, Dad."

Of course, some lessons are harder to learn than others. And it's time, I think, for him to learn a little bit more about the realities of the business world.

"OK, son, let's see your money there. This is how a real business operates. First, you have to pay your mother rent for use of her property."

A blank stare greets this pronouncement.

"Five dollars should cover it."

"But, Dad..."

"And then there's the merchandise. You must pay your suppliers. You don't think lemonade grows on trees, do you, or that brownie mix falls out of the sky? Let's say $3."

My son looks at me accusingly.

"Naturally," I continue, "the transportation costs will add on another $2. And the labor – we helped you make the lemonade and brownies, remember, and you have to pay your employees – will be another $2."

"Two dollars?"

"Apiece."

"But, Dad..."

"Now, now, it's time you learned how things are in the business world. Let's see, we've forgotten the administrative expenses, handling fees and the dividends for the investors. We'll say $3 should do nicely."

"Dad, I don't know about this..."

"And last but certainly not least, you must pay your taxes. That includes the federal, state, Social Security ... I think another $3 should just about cover it."

"Is this for real, Dad?"

"Absolutely, son. You think work is a picnic? You think you get to keep all the money you make? Hah!"

"So how much do I get to keep?"

"Well, let's see what we have left. Add all this up and … hmmm … you're in luck. You have a modest profit margin here. You get to keep this two cents."

"Two cents? Is that all?"

"My advice, son, is to not squander it on frivolities, but you do with it as you see fit."

I see tears welling up in his tender young eyes as this lemonade business starts to turn sour for him.

"Cheer up, son. This is the great free enterprise system at work here."

"I don't think it's very fair," he responds defiantly.

Thus was communism born, I reflect.

"See here," I admonish, "there's another lesson you haven't yet learned about our system of capitalism. Don't be discouraged by this little setback; simply write the government and request a small grant to stimulate the local lemonade industry."

"How much would they give me?" he asks, hope glimmering.

"Probably not a whole lot," I tell him. "Perhaps $5 million to start."

"Really? Five million dollars?"

"Sure, and if that doesn't work, you can always tell them there's a lemonade glut, and the government will end up paying you not to sell it."

"Why would they do that?"

"That lesson is too complicated to get into now," I say. "Maybe later, when you're older."

Kids. They have so much to learn about life.

18 - Government of the People

"I have a big announcement to make," I inform my family at the dinner table.

Blank looks greet me.

"We're going to become a town," I say.

My wife rolls her eyes. The kids kick each other under the table.

"I can see you don't fully comprehend the ramifications of my proposal," I continue unperturbed. "Let me explain. The Smith household is incorporating. Henceforth, we will be known as Smithtown."

"Daddy?" my daughter inquires.

"Yes?"

"Do I have to eat all my potatoes?"

"See here, there are more important matters afoot than vegetative consumption. You kids have just become citizens of a municipality. Do you know what that means?"

"That we get dessert?"

"NO! It means you have to pay taxes."

"What are taxes?" my son wants to know.

"Taxes are money citizens pay in return for certain services. For instance, the town in which you now live will provide you with standard city services, such as water, sewer, security, mass transit, a road - OK, a driveway - network, an administration and finance system, and even recreational facilities."

"But we already have those things," my son points out.

"Yes, but now that we're a town you have to pay for them," I explain patiently. Boy, I wonder, just what is it they're teaching kids in civics classes these days?

"Why?" he persists.

"You think basketballs sprout in the garden, son?"

"Oh."

"So I think that, um, 50 cents a week will just about cover your tax bill."

"But Dad, that's half my allowance!" he wails.

"Welcome to the real world. You know, this can be very instructional for you, preparing you for later in life."

"But Dad..."

"And the first lesson you should learn is that government is bad. It is not only the cause of problems, government is the problem."

"Then why are we becoming one?"

"Good question. And the answer is because we don't want some bureaucrat in some far-off place telling us what we can and cannot do. This is a free country, and if someone is going to pass a bunch of rules and regulations then by golly it should be us who do the passing."

"Does this mean I can set my own bedtime?"

"Don't be an anarchist, son."

"I don't see anything good about being a town," he says petulantly.

"That's because you don't see the big picture. If you were the mayor, like me, you would know that there are a lot of benefits to being in the public sector."

"There are?"

"Sure. We can't operate on your measly tax revenues, you know, so I've already applied for our share of state taxes."

"You mean someone will be sending us money?"

"Of course. This is America, son. We should be getting a check to pave our driveway any day now. We'll get sales tax money every month so we can buy a bunch of stuff. And you won't believe what kind of interest rates we can get when we want to borrow money."

"Daddy," my daughter pipes up. "Can I have a dollar?"

"Not now, sweetie. There's important work to do. Look here, kids, I have a catalog of block grants available from the federal government. Unfortunately, there aren't any available to help pay the cost of educating you guys. We'll just have to struggle on. And son, for you that means no free lunch."

"That's OK, Dad, I don't like the food at school anyway."

"On the other hand, I think I can get Congress to agree to give us a $12 million block grant to use as we see fit for crime prevention, provided we don't play basketball after midnight."

"Gosh, isn't that a lot of money?"

"It's peanuts for governments like us, kids. It's only what's due us. We don't want something for nothing, you know, just our fair share."

"But this doesn't seem right, Dad."

I sigh. Kids just can't grasp the dynamics of modern government.

"It's like this, son. If you get money from the government as a private citizen, it's welfare pure and simple. But if you get it from one government to another, then it's plain old vital spending."

"If you say so."

"Well, it's not just me who says so. It's the way the system works."

I catch myself. Wait, I think, maybe he has a point. Let's think about this.

"You know, you might be right, son. Perhaps this town business is not for us. When you think about it, it's ridiculous for one family to be considered a town."

"So I don't have to call you 'Mayor Dad'?"

"That's right, son. 'Governor Dad' has a much better ring to it."

19 - What's In A Name?

"Dear S. Otj," the letter begins.

S. Otj?

Who the heck, I wonder, is that?

I check the address. It is mine. What is this?

Has some Slovakian or other vowel-impoverished refugee secreted himself in my basement and, unbeknownst to me, established sufficient residency status to feel bold enough to share my mailing address, officially dispensed by no less an authority than the United States Postal Service? If so, then he surely has tapped into my satellite dish down there, too. No wonder I keep getting "Your Polka Hit Parade Live From Prague" on the tube.

But no, there are no aliens in my basement. Just bugs in my junk mail.

I've always been happy with my name: Smith. Yes, it's rather an ordinary one - certainly it's no Otj - but it suits me just fine. No complications, no troubles, only the occasional snide snicker from a motel manager. In fact, the world could do a lot worse than have a few more solid, stolid Smiths in it.

But back to this S. Otj business. The missive, I see, is from one of the primary political parties, soliciting my invaluable opinion on the major issues of the day and ending on a cautionary note as to how civilization as we have known it will surely end without my invaluable contribution to the cause of re-election of the same doddering idiots who have gotten us into this ongoing mess in the first place.

Or words to that effect.

Addressing solicitations of such enduring importance to the republic to a fictitious - not to mention utterly unpronounceable - name makes a citizen ponder, briefly, on the effectiveness and general competence of the solicitor. If the political parties purporting to run this country can't even get your name right while begging for money, it makes you wonder just what else they're getting all wrong.

But then this is exactly the sort of thing those pass-the-bucksters would put down to computer error.

"See here," they would say with all the officiousness they could muster. "It's a simple matter, really. We got the 'S' absolutely right. Anyone can see that. The period is only two keys on a keyboard away from the 'M.' The 'O' abuts the 'I' and there's no question that the 'T' is in the right place. And look here, the 'J' is located hard to starboard of the 'H.' Why, any fool can see that 'S. Otj' is practically the same as 'Smith.'"

I feel better. Especially when I calculate that if the computer had instead shifted a key or two to the left "Smith" might have been mangled into "A Butg."

Then again, I'm not exactly comforted by the possibility that this is the work of some rogue computer, one clearly laboring along a couple of circuits short of a full board, making up names on its own initiative. What kind of dim bulb computers are our government purchasing, anyway? Certainly not inexpensive ones.

And let's not talk about the cost of mailing this weighty junk mail, which includes a lengthy survey by which I may enlighten my leaders as to my particular preferences in public policy. I briefly conjure up an image of my esteemed congressperson, or even the president, taking the time to personally go over my responses. "Hmmm," they will say. "Interesting perspective." Or words to that effect.

The least I can do, I decide, is to fulfill my basic civic responsibility. Especially since the return envelope requires no postage.

The first question is "Sex: Male or Female."

Geez. Why is it that politicians are so hung up on sex? Here's a survey that purports to be a poll designed to assist the leaders of the most powerful nation on the planet in setting public policy and the first question they ask is about my sex life. Those guys - their minds are always in the gutter.

Then again, I muse, perhaps this is a little trick to root out the homosexuals on their mailing list. I check "Female." Then, to demonstrate the deeply held moral values we average citizen types hold, I include in parentheses: "But only with my wife."

That should hold them. But there's trouble anew with number two. They want to know my age.

Well, gosh, do they want me to tell them how old I am - not that they care as long as I'm old enough to vote - or how old this S. Otj is? After all, this correspondence technically is addressed to him, and reading someone else's mail undoubtedly is frowned upon by the Postal Police, if it's not yet barred by a new Constitutional amendment.

I ponder the problem. What are the government form-filling guidelines on this, I wonder. Of course. I put down "Zero to 1," since Mr. S. Otj has existed in some computer bank for less than a year.

"Do you consider your political leanings to be liberal, moderate or conservative?" the survey queries.

I start to put down that I hadn't given it much thought, but notice that there isn't room to write that. Clearly, here is an attempt to categorize me. But what if I don't lean, politically speaking? What if I tilt instead? Or what if S. Otj is, say, an anarchist? Which slot do we put him in?

I put down "All of the above."

There follows a bunch of questions about the president and his performance, Congress and its various shenanigans, economics and taxes, health care and welfare, foreign policy and domestic discomfort, education and immigration.

Pretty dull stuff, so I skip over it.

The last page, I see, gets to the heart of the matter. "Mr. Otj," the letter pleads, "won't you consider giving..."

Ask not what your country can do for you, but how much you can pony up for it. Tough nuts, I think, but old S. Otj doesn't have a credit card to his name. That's the problem with hitting up fictitious people; they may be good for the odd vote, but they usually come up short on the contribution end.

On the other hand, who's to say that Mr. Otj won't soon have a little credit? Surely I'll see this new name turn up on more mail when my pseudoname is sold to the private sector for commercial enterprises. It will make me feel, well, cheap, knowing that a name of mine, even if it isn't really my name, is being auctioned off on some mailing list to the highest bidder. Is this, then, what our great free enterprise system has come to?

Of course it has. So why not go with the flow? Why not play the game? Why not join them if you can't beat them? This is America, after all, and what would any red-blooded all-American person do if given a chance at obtaining a whole new persona? That's right: Become a whole new me. A complete makeover. My new alter ego will be someone more dashing. Someone more debonair. Someone more handsome and witty. Someone who spends a heck of a lot more money than I do.

I can see the form letter in the mail already: "Dear Mr. Otj. You have been carefully screened and selected to receive our credit card with an initial credit of 5 gazillion dollars..."

Graciously, I accept. And send on those catalogs, too. I'll order one of everything. In blue. And say, I never knew those shopping shows could be so much fun. Ship that stuff right out, will you?

And when the stuff comes in the mail, imagine my surprise and indignation at someone's idea of a prank. S. Otj? What kind of silly name is that? Utterly preposterous. The Postal Service Investigatory Division of Criminal Affairs will be notified of this. What kind of fraudulent scheme is this, anyway? Of course, I'll need to keep all this stuff as evidence.

It would work, too, except that the Infernal Revenue Service eventually would hear about this Mr. Otj and his impact on the Gross National Product. Imagine the forms to fill out, the back taxes, the forms to fill out, the audits to attend, the forms to fill out....

So perhaps what I should do is nip this all in the bud and write my congressperson to inform him of my dilemma and head off any potential congressional investigations. I can picture my representative now, opening my letter. I can see him demanding immediate action for a loyal constituent (how will he know I didn't vote for him?). I can even see the computer spitting out a response to my letter.

"Dear Mr. Smith," it will begin. "According to our files, you do not exist. Please be advised that we are aware that the real occupant of this address is a Mr. S. Otj, and that we are taking care of his little problem per his request...."

20 - Helping Out With Homework

It used to be that kids thought homework was a form of cruel and unusual punishment. Now, it's the parents who think that.

Since at my house I am the one who gets to greet the kids when they get home from school, I get the full brunt of the torture.

"So, kids," I say with false enthusiasm. "How was your day? Got a lot of homework?"

"Nah," they chorus in agreement. "Just a little."

"Well?" I prompt, waiting vainly for some enlightenment on the specifics.

They look at me blankly. "Well," my daughter ventures, "can I have a snack?"

"Let's see how much homework we have first," I reply. "What exactly do you have to do?"

My daughter considers the question. "Spelling?" I suggest. She nods her head. "What else?"

"Um, I think that's all, Dad."

Sensing a deterioration in our communication, I proceed to the next logical step here. I rummage in her backpack. "Aha!" I exclaim, holding up a sheet of math problems.

"Oh, yeah," she acknowledges nonchalantly. "I have math, too."

"And you need to do some reading, right?"

"Well, duh, Dad."

I sigh. I direct her to the snack area while I deal with her brother. I get the sense that I'm moving from the rack to the hot pokers in this torture chamber that used to be a living room.

"OK, son, what do you have?"

"I don't have a lot today, Dad." This, naturally, is the answer I was expecting, and I slump disconsolately. I know what "not a lot" means.

"Give it to me straight, son."

He starts pulling books and papers and notebooks out of his backpack. They pile up on the table and he's still conjuring more out of the backpack like a magician pulling rabbits out of a hat.

"Well, let's see," he says as he surveys the teetering pile of schoolwork. "First, I have some math to do."

"What kind of problems are you working on?" I ask. "You may have to get your mom to help you, because you know I don't know much about math. I'm more the word person." I chuckle smugly inwardly.

"They're not problems. I have to write a paper."

"Whoa, son. I'm confused. You have to write a paper for math?"

He nods. "Yeah. Something about why fractions are important or something. It's because we have to get ready for a big writing test later this year."

I shake my head and decide to move on. "What else?"

"Just some social studies."

I flinch. Social studies: the bamboo-under-the-fingernails of homework.

"But it's just reading this chapter and answering these questions."

I don't want to know but I ask anyway. "How many questions?"

"Nineteen."

"Anything else?"

"Nope. Well, there's the long-range social studies project. We're supposed to do a one-page report on every country in the Northern Hemisphere, but we have until the end of next week to do that. You think you could help me with the typing?"

"Gee, I don't know," I say thoughtfully. "You think you could help me take out the garbage and do the laundry?"

"I'll do the typing. Anyway, I have to practice my keyboarding. And the saxophone. Oh yeah, I have to finish that book I'm reading by tomorrow. But don't worry, I've only got 140 pages left."

I groan.

"And I have to do the six sections of my spelling unit by the day after tomorrow. Oh, and we're supposed to read this story and answer this list of 14 questions for language arts."

"Language arts?" I mumble. "What's that?"

"It's reading, Dad," he responds as though I'm some half-wit who flunked out of kindergarten.

"Well, son," I say, "since you have basketball practice in an hour and a half I suggest you get started. Let's tackle this social studies stuff first, OK? I'll help you get started."

I flip through the chapter. "Hmmm. Son, this chapter you're studying, it seems to be on Europe in the Middle Ages, right?"

"Right, Dad."

"Then why do these questions at the back of the chapter have nothing to do with Middle Aged Europe? See here, this first question is asking about the importance of bean curd to the economy of modern Asia. I don't see anything about tofu here in this chapter; it's just all about peasants and feudal lords and manors and stuff."

"Dad," he explains patiently, "they want you to compare concepts. See, they're called 'Compare and Contrast Questions.'"

"I see," I said although I don't. Fortunately, my daughter is back from the kitchen.

"Dad," she says, "is my costume ready?"

"Costume?" I say, dreading what must come next.

"Yes, my costume for Hansel and Gretel. You know, the fairy tale. I'm supposed to dress up like Gretel for school tomorrow."

"And who might be dressing up as Hansel?" I ask faintly.

"Dad!" She taps her foot with her hands on her hips. "Mom said you would do it."

I bury my head in my hands. Where is the government when you need it, I wonder. You spend all these tax dollars, and what services do parents get? Free education, hah! How come there's not a full-blown federal Department of Homework Assistance? How come there's no toll-free homework hotline to help you out? I mean, what is Congress doing up there when it's not investigating, er, health, as they would call it in school?

"Dad," my daughter interrupts my reverie. "We also need to start on the castle."

"Castle?" I hear myself ask.

"Yes, didn't I tell you? I need to make a castle out of plywood, with a working drawbridge because it's also going to be a birdhouse. My teacher says parents can help make it if they want. Especially if we use power tools."

My son speaks up now. "That reminds me, Dad, do you happen to have an extra particle accelerator lying around in the workshop?"

I look at my first-born and wonder at what time has wrought. "A particle accelerator? No, I don't think so. I think I threw our last one away. Silly me, I couldn't imagine what use it might be. By the way, what the heck is a particle accelerator and why do you need one?"

"For my science project. We need to put together a fully-functioning scientific model of some kind."

I rub my forehead. I count to 10. I go on to 20. I consider if it's too early for a little liquid snack. I take a deep breath. "And when, exactly, is this project due?"

"Um, tomorrow."

"Son," I say calmly, for I am beyond pain now, or soon will be, "have you ever heard the one about the dog eating your homework?"

"What?"

"Never mind."

21 - *The Dumbing Down Of Dad*

When did I get to be so stupid?

I mean, I used to be smart. I made good grades in school. (OK, there was that problem with geometry in ninth grade, but that can be blamed more on the distraction otherwise known as the length of Jennifer McElroy's mini-skirt than on any inherent shortcomings with parallelograms and pi.) I went to college. I kept up to date on issues important to civilization as we knew it. So if I wasn't exactly an intellectual, neither was I an illiterate with all the mental capacity of a warthog and the attention span of a toaster oven.

But somehow over the years I've dumbed down. Been stupidicized. And I don't have a clue how it happened.

There was a time when I was an outright genius, at least in my own home. I was Super Dad; my kids were convinced that I had all the answers. Which is saying a lot considering how many questions they asked when they were younger. Dad knew everything - and what he didn't know, of course, he made up.

I could even perform astonishing feats of magic. For instance, I could amaze my young children while driving with my mysterious ability to turn on the reflectors embedded in the middle of the road by surreptitiously flicking on the car's headlights. Now the only magic my kids are interested in is seeing how quickly they can make money disappear.

Boy, are they good at that.

No longer do my kids have blinding faith in everything I say, blithely accepting as gospel every explanation and every answer to every question. I began to notice a couple of years ago a bit of skepticism creeping in on their part when I was rounding out their education, a blip in their belief system in the infallibility of dad's knowledge. Puzzled frowns began to replace wide-eyed acceptance. Nods of understanding became furrowed brows of contemplation. And then outright smirks and snickers took over as the kids would look at each other as if to say, "Dad's pulling our legs again because he doesn't know what he's talking about."

Such as when one of my kids asked me why it is we drive on the right side of the road, while people in some other countries drive on the left.

"Well," I say, rubbing my chin to signal the impending appearance of thoughtful wisdom, "it all goes back to the American Revolution, you know. We were rebelling from England, and the British drive on the left, so we wanted to, you know, rebel from their laws and rules, so the Founding Fathers decided that here in America we would do just the opposite and drive on the right side."

"But, Dad, they didn't have cars back in those days."

"No cars? Of course not. I knew that. But they had, um, carts and, uh, carriages. And wagons. You know, if you'd study history more closely, you'd know all this stuff. I think it's a clause in the Constitution, about the right side."

"You mean an amendment."

"A what?"

"An amendment. The Constitution has amendments."

"Yes, yes, I know that. But the driving on the right thing is a clause. They didn't think it needed a whole amendment, like free speech and the right to be incompetent, so they gave it just a clause."

"But..."

"I tell you what," I say and bring out the sure-fire argument clincher. "Don't take my word for it. Look it up yourself."

Naturally, they can't be bothered to actually look it up themselves, but the seed of doubt is planted. Skepticism rears its ugly head. And Dad's IQ is ratcheted down a notch or two.

I blame much of this rising level of stupidity on my part to the modern education system. Not my education – my children's. After all, it's in school that kids begin to learn to question their parents' omniscience. I think it was at about the fifth-grade level that I started in on the excuses for not helping with homework: "Um, son, I'm not sure I can help you with that math there because, um, you know, this is the new math and what I studied was the old math. We didn't do it the same way and I, er, wouldn't want you to learn it the wrong way."

"But, Dad, this is just long division."

"Right. Long division. But, see, when I took math, we did it the short way."

"The short way?"

"Yes, you know, like opposite the long way."

"But..."

"Son, trust me on this. You can ask your mother for help with math when she gets home. I'm pretty sure she learned it the long way."

The eye-rolling is a sure tip-off that they're not exactly buying into this explanation.

Even when I felt I was on firmer ground, I realized what a slippery slope this education stuff could be. I figured as a writer I could at least help my children learn to express themselves through words, but I soon discovered that I write all wrong for classroom purposes.

"Well, here's a problem right here," I would tell one of my kids as I helped edit some pre-practice take-home evaluation cognitive learning assistance testing mechanism. "Your paragraphs are way too long. You don't need five sentences in every paragraph."

"Yes, you do, Dad. My teacher says so."

"Well, your teacher is … not entirely correct. I mean, not all paragraphs have to be that long."

"Yes, they do. My teacher says they'll take off points if each paragraph isn't written exactly like that."

"That may be, but I write paragraphs that aren't that long all the time. In fact, very few of my paragraphs reach such length."

"Then you'd fail the writing test in my class."

There go the eyes again. Rolling.

"Well," I say, desperate now, "writing shouldn't be so regimented. It's about creative expression. If you can say everything you want to say in a paragraph in three sentences, or even two, then there's nothing wrong with that."

"Dad?"

"Yes?"

"Is this like that short long division?"

I reflect on all this as my first-born goes off to high school. High school! I mean, I was just in high school – well, it doesn't seem that long ago. How can my son be in high school already? What happened to those days of pre-school, of kindergarten, of green eggs and ham, Ninja Turtles and Matchbox cars?

High school is scary stuff. C'mon, we all remember high school and what it does to you. It changes you forever. Who among us can honestly say they didn't graduate from high school a completely different person than the one who first walked the

halls? I mean, just think of all the things you learn in high school
– and I'm not talking about the stuff they teach in class.

Is it any wonder I have trouble sleeping at night? That I
wake up in a cold sweat wondering if he is going to do the same
things I did in high school? Make the same mistakes? Have the
same crises? Concentrate on the wrong shapes in geometry class?

And of course the end of childhood is in view now. High
school is finite; it has a time limit. Four years and you're out of
here, kid. Then it will be time to leave the nest. Make it on your
own. Pack up your stuff and head off for college or wherever.
Say goodbye. Rent the room out.

Four more years.

Oh, my.

Imagine what an idiot I'll be by then.

22 - *How Do You Spell Tax Relief?*

"Hello, Infernal Revenue Service. How may we make life hell for you?"

"Er, um, yes. I was calling about that tax cut the president promised."

"Ah, yes. We've been getting a lot of calls about that."

"I can imagine. I was calling to see just how much of a tax cut I am going to get. Can you help me?"

"Of course, sir. That's what the new, friendly IRS is all about: Helping taxpayers pay their fair share and then some. So let's see, now. The first thing we have to do is see if you qualify."

"Qualify? I thought this tax cut was across the board. You know: It applies to everyone."

"How quaint. But, really, sir, you know how politicians are. They say the darnedest things."

"I see."

"So, let's begin, shall we? Now, just how large of a contribution did you make to the president's campaign?"

"Er, contribution? I didn't make any political contributions."

"Oh, dear."

"Is that a problem?"

"Not for us. But just let me make a quick note here for Cummings over in audits. All right. Now, then, would you say that your income puts you in the billionaire class?"

"You're kidding, right?"

"Just asking, sir. Ten-figure earnings would entitle you to an automatic rebate from your government."

"Really? Billionaires get money back from the government? What's the rationale behind that?"

"Well, sir, isn't it obvious? They do so much for the economy. Rebates are a way for the government to express its thanks for all they do."

"Kind of a payback for a payoff, that sort of thing?"

"Your government would never phrase it so crudely, sir."

"Well, I don't pay off politicians and I'm not a billionaire. Does that mean I don't qualify for a tax cut after all?"

"Not necessarily, sir. Are you currently or have you in the past calendar year been a large international corporation or cartel?"

"Not to my knowledge."

"I'll put that down as a 'Not a Potential Political Contributor.' Are you currently or have you in the past calendar year employed lobbyists in Congress or other branches of government?"

"Um, no. Hey, wait a minute. Does writing your congressperson count?"

"Only if there was a check enclosed."

"Never mind, then."

"To be honest, sir, it's not looking good, tax cut-wise. You certainly aren't helping your own cause here."

"What can I say? I'm just your average taxpayer. I just thought we were the ones getting some relief."

"Well, just what is your adjustable gross income?"

"Ah, let's just say I'm in the average income category. I'm pretty typical, you know: married, the standard two kids, regulation issue dog and cat. Is there any chance I'd be eligible for any type of tax cut?"

"Hang on a moment, sir, and let me do some calculations … hmmm, average middle class … yes, here you go. Actually, you would be getting a tax rebate."

"Really? That's great? About how much?"

"Well, sir, this is a rough estimate, and you would need to get an expert tax preparer to figure the exact amount, but by our calculations you would be receiving a net tax relief in the neighborhood of 12 cents."

"Twelve cents? As in 12 pennies? That's a pretty low-rent neighborhood."

"Sir, an across-the-board tax reduction means everybody who pays in gets something back. You can't expect everybody to get back everything they pay in. Why, your government would be out of business. Twelve cents would be your percentage of the overall tax cut."

"Wow. I won't know where to spend all that. A Ferrari or a Corvette, hmmm, that's a tough choice."

"Sir, if I may say so, sarcasm does not become you."

"Jeez, 12 cents. So that's it? That's all I'm getting back out of, what, a trillion-dollar tax cut?"

"Oh, I don't know, sir. You could always die."

"Excuse me?"

"Die. Perish. Pass on. Expire. There's considerable savings in death."

"Death? What are you talking about? I should die?"

"The estate tax, sir. The president would eliminate it. So you could save a bundle for your descendants by dying."

"No, thanks. I think I'll pass."

"Suit yourself, sir."

"So, just out of curiosity, how is the government planning to pay for these billions in tax cuts?"

"That's really not my department, sir. We just collect the money."

"I mean, I don't see where any spending cuts are planned. So it just stands to reason that if you cut income without cutting spending, you're going to run out of money."

"Ha, ha, sir. Very funny. That bit about 'reason' applying to your government. How droll."

"So you're saying that the government doesn't have to play by the same economic rules as the rest of us?"

"Sir, you're talking about the institution that prints money."

"Let me see if I've got this straight. The government is giving out this huge tax cut – to certain people and businesses – but is not going to reduce spending, so the deficit will start ballooning again. Doesn't this sound familiar?"

"Déjà vu all over again, or something like that, sir?"

"Yeah. I mean, isn't this a prescription for financial disaster?"

"So you're saying you're against tax cuts? In that case, let me transfer you over to Simmons in electronic filing. He'll be happy to lead you step by step through the process of paying us on-line. Or you could just have your employer mail us your check. It's pretty much the same difference."

"No, no, no. I didn't say I was against tax cuts. I'm all for tax cuts. Especially if I'm getting one. But, hey, 12 cents? C'mon. It's obvious the ol' middle class is getting stuck again."

"Well, sir, the only other thing I can suggest, if you really want to increase your tax decrease, is to increase your income."

"You're saying I should go make more money so I can get a bigger tax cut?"

"Absolutely."

"But if I made more money, I wouldn't need a tax cut."

"Well, sir, there you go. Sounds to me like another satisfied customer."

23 - Don't Just Stand There

No loitering.

You've seen the signs. They've sprouted up here and there, stern warnings urging you on your way, to keep moving, to be about your business. Subtle reminders that you might be moving too slowly in this fast-paced world, so pick up the pace or you risk being out of step.

So we hustle and bustle on, fearfully glancing around lest we be accused of being some sort of malingering, subversive lawbreaker; as respectable citizens we no longer sneer and scoff at what surely must be duly enacted ordinances by our elected representatives. Maturity has taught us to frown on rebellion, revolution, contrariness and other similar products of youthful exuberance.

This assumes, of course, that these signs have been erected at the people's command. Are there really elected boards and bodies out there deliberating and debating and then formally directing that tax dollars be spent on the construction and erection of signs reminding the citizenry that it is against the law to stand around?

I wonder who actually petitioned the government to address this particular issue. Was it pedestrians intimidated by boorish street gangs hanging out on the sidewalks making nuisances of themselves by being in the way? Are merchants staring out their shop windows thinking to themselves: "If those loiterers would just get moving, they might come in here and buy a bunch of stuff and, with my profit margin, I can take that trip to Hawaii this Christmas after all?"

Or did the government come up with this idea all on its own? After all, the government places limits on how fast we can go, so why not on how slowly as well? I suspect the government is prodding us into action so that we're constantly moving, accomplishing something, and contributing to the economy because if we taxpayers are simply standing around being unproductive members of society it isn't making any money off us.

The irony, here, of course, is that the government is the biggest bunch of loiterers around. That's what the government is made up of: Professional loiterers. Shuffling papers, conducting meetings, attending conferences, appointing committees, preparing studies, spending other people's money – this is world-class wheel-spinning, not productive activity. Wouldn't we be better off if the entire government bureaucracy quit pretending it was being productive and just went and hung out on the street corner all day?

And just how does the government define loitering, anyway? There's a pretty fine line between appearing to do nothing and seeming to do something. Does window-shopping count as a fruitful activity or a waste of time and space? What if you're standing on the sidewalk because you don't remember where you parked your car; is this simple forgetfulness or criminal behavior?

What if you're a thief hanging about suspiciously, and a police officer comes along and tells you to move along and you say, "Hey, excuse me, officer, I am not some petty loiterer but a professional criminal who is at this moment in time engaged in casing the bank across the street, an activity requiring a certain amount of expertise in the art of surveillance. So if you will excuse me, I would like to get back to work." Does the cop apologize because, unlike loitering, bank casing preparatory to the actual criminal activity is not illegal, per se?

Since loitering is against the law, you have to figure that there must be some penalty for it. Is there a fine? Do you really get hauled into court where a judge pounds his gavel and orders you to cough up $50 because you weren't moving fast enough? What must all the motorists hanging out in court waiting to contest their speeding tickets think about this?

Can you get jail time if you are a repeat offender? Do these exchanges take place in prisons around the country:

"Hey, punk, whatcha in for?"

"Er, uh, loitering. Sir."

"Loitering, huh? You sleazebag. Do you know what we do to loiterers and litterers here in the joint?"

Is crime really so under control now that law enforcement agencies have the time and resources to spend tracking down loiterers? Next we'll be seeing police departments training special loitering SWAT teams; there you'll be, just hanging out and whiling away the hours, and suddenly 14 heavily armed, highly trained strike team members will have surrounded you, pointing the business ends of some high-powered laser-guided handheld tactical nuclear missile launchers at various vulnerable parts of your body.

No doubt the FBI, CIA, DEA and several other acronyms are, as we speak, launching an all-out War on Loitering, complete with a Loitering Czar who reports to the president, when he's not waging his own judicial battles.

Expect our children to be forced to endure anti-loitering programs in school. And imagine the judicial system clogged with loitering cases, which in turn will cause - horrors - law schools to increase their class sizes to handle the load.

Is this what our government wants? Apparently so. Towns seem pleased as punch with their "No Loitering" signs. They may as well put up more signs saying, "We're a Town on the Move" or "People Don't Hang Out Here." Although I can't imagine what "Don't Stop Here or Even Slow Down Because You'll Be Arrested" would do for the tourism industry.

The problem with all this hurrying about is that we've lost sight of the fact that we're already moving too fast. Whatever happened to simple relaxation and contemplation? People ought to slow down, hang out, do nothing, think about the beauty of life. What's wrong with stopping and looking around, taking in the scenery, watching the world go by?

My advice is to move at your own pace. And next time you see a "No Loitering" sign, be a rebel.

24 – It's All In The Numbers

Sometimes it's the little things in life that are so aggravating. Like addresses.

Addresses are extremely personal things. I don't have yours; you don't have mine. They may be similar, but never identical. They are one of the few things in life we can count on to be unique.

So when the government arbitrarily changes them, it's not something to be taken lightly. It was a chilling reminder of the capricious power of government when the letter arrived at my house coldly informing me that my long-time address would henceforth be obsolete.

This being the government, however, the missive naturally was mailed to my old address.

I was, to say the least, distressed at this infringement of a citizen's most basic of all property rights. I briefly pondered insurrection, but since an address change is not the stuff to inspire revolution, I instead called my congressperson.

"Sorry, the congressman is not in at this particular moment in time," I was told. "He's off looking out for your interests, fighting wasteful spending and big government on your behalf."

"Gee," I reply, "I thought you guys *were* the government."

"Well, technically speaking, you would be correct in your assumption. However, I would be happy to mail you at no charge the congressman's position paper on that. We have free mailing, you know."

"Free for whom? Never mind; I don't think I'd be interested in any mailing. As a matter of fact, I was hoping to talk to my congressperson or a reasonable facsimile thereof with just such a problem."

"Hey, that's what we're here for. Um, say, you did vote in the last election, didn't you?"

"The last election? Vote? Oh, sure, sure. Listen, this is about my address. The government here has up and changed it."

"How odd, sir. They singled out your house to change the address?"

"Well, not exactly. They changed a lot of them. Something about it being more convenient for emergency services. You know, so they'd know which house was on fire and stuff like that."

"Wouldn't that be the one with the flames and smoke coming out of it?"

"That's what I thought. But this is supposed to be more efficient or something."

"So what's the problem?"

"Was there a public referendum on this? I don't think so. Did they ask us if we wanted new addresses? No. Worse, I'm being told in great detail just how I'm supposed to display my new address. They even gave me the numbers in the politically correct size: 3 ½ inches. And reflective. They have to be visible from the road, unless you're like me and your door isn't visible from the road, in which case I have to put them on a post I have to erect out by the road. I ask you, have you ever heard anything as bureaucratic as that?"

"You don't deal with the IRS on a regular basis, do you?"

"Um, no. So what can you do about this? I feel this is petty government intrusion. I thought Congress was out to restore personal freedom and unchain us from the shackles of big government."

"Nice turn of the phrase there, sir. And unshackling government chains is what we're all about. Why, even as we speak, Congress is working hard to limit government interference in the lives of you, the people, and eliminate pesky government rules and regulations."

"Really? Such as?"

"Such as requirements that you drink clean water. This Congress believes that in America, people have a right to drink dirty water if they so choose."

"They do?"

"Absolutely."

"Let me get this straight. You're saying I can turn my property into a toxic waste dump without so much as a permit provided I have the proper address properly posted?"

"In a manner of speaking, yes. And Congress is working to rid America of plenty of other intrusive obligations, as well."

"It is?"

"Sure. For instance, poor people should have a right to get a job, free of any government burden that would automatically give them something to eat and make them vote in a liberal fashion. And certainly children have a fundamental right to the best education the states can afford, free of federal interference and spending, don't you think?"

"Look, getting back to my address problem … the ironic thing is that my driveway is in such bad shape I'm not sure anyone would want to drive up it to even see my new posted address even if it did meet these stringent government standards."

"If you're fishing about for a road improvement grant, sir, I'm afraid you're barking up the wrong tree. Our records show that your campaign contribution levels don't qualify you…"

"No, no, no. Don't worry, I'm not looking for a handout. Simple justice will do. I just don't understand why I have to put up with petty bureaucratic interference in my own home."

"And you don't, sir. This is America, after all, a free country. Your congressman will hear about this personally, I can assure you. And I know he will want to investigate this matter, perhaps even convening a special subcommittee or embarking on an extensive fact-finding mission throughout the greater Caribbean…"

"But I don't live in the Caribbean."

"No matter, there are still many facts to be found down there. As I was saying, after he investigates this matter, he will write to you personally of his findings and conclusions."

"Really? He'd do that?"

"You bet. There's just one thing. To better facilitate the delivery of this important piece of congressional mailing…"

"Yes?"

"Make sure those numbers on your address are at least 3 ½ inches high, OK?"

Part IV

Fun And Games

25 - Recreation Can Be Relentless

In this fast-paced age of non-stop stress, it's important to occasionally slow down, to refresh body and mind through some amusing diversion. And what better way to relax than to partake of some recreational activity?

My favorite form of recreation employs minimal accoutrements: a lounge chair, a deck, perhaps a frothy refreshment or two. Peace and quiet would be nice, but those two commodities are rare at my house.

"Dad?" My daughter interrupts my reverie.

"Yes, sweetie, what is it?" I am primed for some serious recreating here, but patience, as they say, is a virtue, so I am the epitome of responsive parenthood.

"It's time to go."

"Go? Where on earth would we go? We have everything we need right here." To reassure her that she has my undivided attention I pry open one eye.

"To dance."

"Dance?"

"Yes, Dad," she says with exasperation, tapping her foot to indicate that at an early age she has already figured out that dads are men and men are, well, not quite up to the standards women expect in the organizational department. "I have dance today. Duh."

Dance class. Of course. How could I forget? I glance at my watch. Twelve minutes. Plenty of time. It's only 10 minutes away. I cast one last look at my lounge chair. Ah, the brief moments we spent together...

Into the car we go. "C'mon son," I say, "we've got to get going."

"All ready, Dad."

"How come you have your baseball stuff with you?" I ask, but I already know the answer.

"Because we have baseball practice later. Jeez, dad, you're the coach, don't you remember?"

Right. The coach. Yes, I remember everything clearly now. I remember my wife telling me, "It'll be fun, honey. You have to go to all the practices and games anyway, so you might as well be doing something while you're there." Oh, yes, she was very encouraging. And where is she now? Huh? No doubt she'll have some flimsy excuse like she's at work, while I'm here hustling rugrats all over creation.

"Mom's picking me up after dance, Dad," my daughter announces, as though she is reading my thoughts.

"She is?"

"Yes. So I can go to T-ball practice."

"T-ball? You're playing T-ball this year? Why can't I take you when we go to baseball practice?"

"'Cause it's not at the same place."

"Right," I say. "I knew that."

At dance, I see someone who looks vaguely familiar. "Hey," I say, "I know you. Aren't you my wife?"

"Sorry," she says, "no time for chit-chat."

"OK, I'll see you after practice at home."

"No, you won't."

"I won't?"

"You're forgetting Scouts."

"I am?"

"Yes. We have Brownies and Boy Scouts tonight."

"But when do we eat?"

She chuckles at that notion. "We're dieting, remember?"

"Right. So, we'll skip supper and rendezvous back at the ranch at, oh, 9 o'clock. OK?" Which will be just in time to get the kids in bed. Late. Again.

Off to baseball practice. We arrive, almost on time, and my blood pressure is not too bad considering it took 18 minutes to drive two miles because a lone tourist was quite taken with our beautiful scenery on our winding country roads. Only people with no children drive that slowly.

The team is waiting. They have been taking turns practicing slides in the mud puddle by third base. Fortunately I am the coach and not the team laundry man.

I get them to stop sliding, and they jump right into batting practice, which entails each of them swinging a bat and seeing how close to each other's heads they can get. I get them out in the field to minimize personal injury.

Jimmy or Johnny or Jesse is tugging at my shirt. "Can I pitch, coach?"

"Sure, um, son." What is this kid's name? "Give it a whirl."

He winds up, his body twisting into positions that would amaze a contortionist. It is painful to watch. He completes his windup and flings the ball. It whizzes by the head of the on-deck batter, a mere 30 feet from home plate.

"Oops," he says.

"Son," I say, "that's quite an arm you have there. Perhaps you'd be better suited for the outfield."

"But my dad says I should be a pitcher."

I sigh. "Has your dad ever played catch with you?"

"Once."

"Once?"

"Yeah. He was pretty upset about the window."

"The window? Never mind; it's best I don't know."

I hit ground balls to the team. The first one goes through the legs of the shortstop. The left fielder assumes a defiant attitude because of his exile to this grassy outpost of the baseball world. He crosses his arms and refuses to field the ball. A passive protest that would make Gandhi proud, and I wonder why my coach's training did not include a symposium on labor-management disputes.

The shortstop retrieves the ball. "Cover second," I yell, and 12 kids dutifully charge second base and end up in a pile of legs and arms in the dirt. I turn away from the carnage. Can they fire a volunteer coach, I wonder?

Mercifully, practice ends. Hop in the car, and we're only 20 minutes late for the Scout meeting. "Dad," my son says, "I forgot to tell you, but I have homework tonight."

"Homework?" I yell, swerving to pass some plodding Lincoln that's only doing 55. "How can you think of school work at a time like this?" I catch myself. Hmmm, I think. Some time I need to sit down and rethink my priorities.

The problem, I realize, is that recreation is too relentless. Perhaps we've organized our fun too much. When I was a kid, we had Little League, sure, and Boy Scouts, but I don't remember my parents hauling me off everywhere. I remember pickup games, making up the rules with the neighborhood kids and whiling away the hours recreating with nary a parent in sight. This must be what it's like to give your kids what you never had.

"So, son, what will you be doing at your Scout meeting tonight?"

"We're going to plan our hiking trip this weekend, Dad."

"Hiking? That sounds like fun."

"Oh, by the way, they need a couple of parents to go along. I said you'd probably go. Will yah, Dad, please? It'll be fun."

Visions of a weekend on my deck fade. "Sure," I hear myself saying. Why not? Some father-son bonding. Quality time here in the pre-teens. Gotta grab it while you can. "How far are we hiking?" I ask casually.

"Just 10 miles this time."

"Ten miles?"

"Yeah. And then we're gonna camp."

"Camp? We're going to camp after the hike?"

"Yeah. Cool, huh?"

"Camping? Oh, boy, that will be fun," I lie, mentally comparing the relative creature comforts of my nice, soft bed in a cozy room with its own bathroom against a damp sleeping bag on the cold, hard ground with the bathroom somewhere in the dark bushes.

Later, much later, my wife and I finally plop down to rest. The kids are finished recreating for the day, they've been tucked in, and are sleeping quietly.

"You know, it's been a hectic day," I say, trying to sound philosophical but knowing that it's coming off more like a whine, "but the good news is that soon this week will be over, and the next one has got to be better. Surely next week will be more relaxing."

"Dear," my wife says sweetly, "the kids start swimming lessons next week."

26 - Boorish Behavior Strikes Out

Ah, fall is in the air. It's the season of colorful leaves, frosty mornings, warm fires and, of course, the Fall Classic itself, the World Series.

This is one of those spectacular sporting events that even non-sports fans watch. It's a chance for people all over the world to see the glorious pageantry of a dramatic extravaganza that is quintessentially American.

Not to mention the dazzling displays of professional spitting and major league crotch-grabbing.

What is it with baseball players? What is it about picking up an overstuffed glove or a large rounded stick that inspires a person to spit incessantly while continually rearranging extremely personal body parts?

I know these are some of the hoary traditions that baseball purists are always nattering on about, the time-honored customs that they claim make America's pastime so unique – such as the one that makes some septuagenarian coach wear a uniform as though he were about to leap out of the dugout at any moment and lay down a bunt.

Why don't other sports adopt this custom? Basketball coaches could save fortunes by exchanging those expensive suits they sweat through for some shorts and a sleeveless jersey. And football coaches should have to wear pads, a helmet and those little pants that barely reach their knees.

Anyway, where do baseball players learn spitting and crotch-grabbing? Certainly not from their mothers; I bet there are a lot of moms out there who wince every time they see their sons playing big league baseball: "Good lord, Junior, wipe your chin, and how many times have I told you not to do that in public?"

And what are you supposed to do when your kids start emulating their heroes? "But, Dad, I saw these guys on TV doing it – and people were cheering them!"

"I don't care, son, you're not supposed to spit on the carpet."

"But, Dad, those guys make $14 gazillion a year."

"OK, son, just don't let your mother see you do it."

The least television could do is broadcast warnings to viewers: "Attention, some pretty rude, crude and generally unattractive behavior is coming up next, so be sure to stay in your seat unless you feel your sensibilities might be offended." But then the networks would run the risk that some parents might not let their kids watch America's game, which sometimes isn't over until 12:30 in the morning.

Boorish behavior may seem like a minor matter, but this is how you chart the decline of morality and civilization as we know it. For gosh sakes, if you're going to allow some guy to grab his, er, groin area (as it's technically referred to by such experts as TV announcers) in full view of the nation and the world during prime time, can full-frontal nudity be far behind?

Television should do a better job of not glorifying gratuitous crotch-grabbing and excessive bodily discharges. Are we supposed to simply ignore this behavior, pretend we didn't see it? What makes conduct that is generally frowned upon in polite society be perfectly all right if done on artificial grass in a stadium filled with people and in front of television cameras? If TV had characters in regular programs acting in this manner, you can be sure that the Association of Expectoration Opponents or the League of Public Decency (Body Parts Division) would be all over them like a wet T-shirt.

What would happen if everyone conducted themselves at their workplaces as do ball players? Can you see a corporate executive spitting on the Persian rug in the conference room before getting down to business with the board? Would you want your waitperson at a restaurant to do this before taking your order? Can you see a salesman tugging at his pants before he steps up to make a pitch?

What if the president started doing this type of stuff before a major televised address to Congress? "My fellow Americans ... ptoooey ... ding! Yo, good catch with that spittoon, uh, senator." (Grab, grab.) "Now, ah, we need to seize this moment to, um, hold on to our prosperity..."

Of course, women are not immune to rearrangement of body parts, either. Consider bathing suits; women are constantly tucking in here and pulling out there. What is it with the swimsuit industry? You pay $145 for something with less raw material in it than your average washcloth and it doesn't even adhere properly when you move? Is there, by chance, some design flaw here?

Perhaps that's all baseball players need: New fashions and a lesson in appropriate oral etiquette. Some baggy pants might help, and then let them stay after the game to mop up the field.

Yes, it's time to clean up the national pastime. It is corrupting America's youth, undermining our sense of right and wrong, eroding our values, subverting our morals and affecting our bottom line.

When you watch the World Series, you too no doubt will be offended by this dreadful behavior. Good. Get angry. Write to the TV executives. Write to the congressperson of your choice. Write to your senators. Write to your president. Tell them you resent people hawking up juicy ones and grabbing their crotches in your living room.

And tell them you're so mad you could ... well, spit.

27 - Dreaming Of The Olympics

Watching the Olympics, I feel myself becoming numb. Unfortunately, it's not from excitement.

Actually, I find that what I'm really watching are Olympic commercials. A seemingly endless array of products march across my television screen, each a gold medal winner drubbing the competing brands.

Look: There's the toilet bowl cleaner of choice for our Olympic bobsled team. And here's what our figure skaters use to prevent ugly underarm stains from wiping out a perfect score. And that's the soda pop all our world-class athletes guzzle while training rigorously to be the best they can be.

I sit astonished, much as I would if watching some mere mortal soar off a ski jump and glide magically through the air – a scene I can only picture in my mind instead of on the screen as the announcer has been cheerfully promising that it will be "coming up next" for the last two hours.

Here, wait, an actual Olympic event is about to occur. We're in an ice skating rink, only now they call it a pavilion or some such thing. The stands are full. Flags are waving. Judges are judging. And the ice skaters are ... dancing? It sure doesn't look like any ice skating I've ever seen. It sure looks like they're dancing. With ice skates. On the ice.

I flop back in my chair. I cannot hide my disappointment. Why are they dancing on the ice? With music. The rules on this are pretty clear, I thought: It's not a sport if you do it with music. Music is played at halftimes, or before the event, or even during timeouts. But not during the event. That crosses the line and makes it something else entirely.

Since when did this ice dancing stuff become an Olympic sport, anyway? Do they have dancing in the Summer Games, with fierce competition in the tango and the samba? I can't believe I didn't see the country line dancing finals at the last Olympics; the cowboy hats would have been hard to miss. Are there even now Olympic dance hall training facilities being constructed in communities across the world as aspiring Olympians try out the Tennessee two-step with visions of glory in their heads at later Games?

I shudder to think. But we all have our dreams, I suppose. Mine right now is to see an actual Olympic event being contested, live and not on tape delay, preferably involving skiers jumping off the side of a mountain. You don't do that, I'm sure, with Muzak blaring in your ears.

Instead, I'm watching an emotional feature on a perky, plucky young lass from Oakwood, Iowa, who since the age of 3 has been training to be an Olympic cross-country skier and has endured countless personal tragedies, such as the time she had to skip her senior prom to practice.

I'm dozing off now as I await the ski jumping, dreaming that the next Winter Games are being held in my little mountain town, and I'm renting out my house to some rich fat cat for $5,000 a day while I practice water skiing in Jamaica and wondering why that isn't an Olympic sport. Hey, mon, the water's not even frozen.

I'm rudely brought back to reality by the official beer industry's sponsor of the Olympic Games. This, I assume, is what all the top-notch skiers quaff just before heading down the slopes at 120 mph.

Now here's an item of interest. We're strolling around the Olympic Village, looking at the snow. There's an ice sculpture. There's a big mound of snow. There's the scenic views of the mountains. Oops, it's just a credit card commercial. They only take one kind of credit card at the Olympics?

The announcer is back. He's saying something about ski jumping. I sit up. This is it. Here we go. Ski jumping is coming up next ... right after this feature on a perky, plucky young lad from Oakdale, Indiana, who ever since he rode a sled down a hill at age 5 has wanted to be an Olympic luge champion.

He, however, has had to overcome amazing adversity, including the fact that no one in his hometown knows what a luge is. No matter, he has devoted his entire life at great personal sacrifice – no fast food or video games for our boy – to the luge, and even though he finished 48th and has absolutely no future since his skill, riding a sled, is not exactly in great demand on the job market, his is still a great story, isn't it?

I yawn. Time is running out for the ski jumping event. Surely it is next. No, after these commercial messages we're out on some ski trail, watching cross-country skiers, which is about as exciting as watching snow melt. What is that they're all carrying? Those look like guns. Yes, now they're stopping and shooting. Ye gods, are they shooting at each other? This is what I call ruthless competition. But, no, they're shooting at targets. They have something on their ears; perhaps they're listening to music. Now they're skiing some more. What kind of sport is this?

We're yanked back to the ice skating rink. At least this time they're skating instead of hopping around. Gee, those are awfully skimpy costumes. Aren't contestants in sporting events supposed to wear uniforms? This is more like a swimsuit competition on ice. Aren't those poor girls cold? How come the guys aren't wearing swimsuits, too, I wonder.

The announcer is telling me not to look. I look. And see flashing on the screen the names of who won the gold, silver and bronze for the ski jumping, which they will show in its near-entirety – tomorrow at 6 a.m.

I'm drifting off again. In my dreams, I hear my son proclaim his intention to one day be an Olympic athlete. I smile with pride. I can see him grinning as he smashes world records. I can see him clutching a gold medal, waving to the world on global television.

And I can see the story they will air at some future Olympics about the plucky young athlete who had to overcome such great hardship and adversity: His father, who one night leaped high off his reclining chair, floated through the air as though suspended in time, and made a picture-perfect gold-medal landing with both feet smacking right into the TV set.

28 - Learning About The Game Of Life

It was every boy's dream, or nightmare: Two outs, bases loaded, the bottom of the last inning, the team is down by a run. Three balls, two strikes. The next pitch brings glorious success or tormented failure, for this is Little League baseball — all the world a young boy needs is bounded by the far horizon of the outfield fence.

I grip my bat in sweaty hands and paw at the dirt with cleated feet. No slugger am I, no graceful athlete, but this is my one big chance for elusive glory and adulation. The pitcher throws, the crowd cheers, the ball flies toward me ... and I gasp with relief as it sails by low. I walked, I think, I did not fail, but then like Casey I hear "strike three!"

Such are the bittersweet memories of youth. That was the last year I ever played organized sports; the next year we moved, and by then it seemed my peers had moved much farther on in athletic ability, and anyway other interests developed, other needs arose.

But my son from an early age has shown a keen desire for sports, and unlike me a surprising ability as well. Unfortunately, I seem to have passed on to him a fear of failure, and I wonder how he will handle the unavoidable ravages of defeat. So it is that an ominous dread tinges my excitement and pride as I await his first real game of Little League.

I shift nervously on my feet as he approaches the plate for the first time. I yell encouragement, for I am both parent and coach. I still marvel at my acceptance of this latter responsibility — me, the no-hit bench-warming wonder, now the expert master of all the stratagems of the game. Am I living out my sports fantasies through my son? Psychologists would say so, no doubt, but I never cared much for their expert analyses of hidden motives and unfulfilled desires. I just want my son and his friends to understand that sports, particularly at an early age, do not have to be so rigidly and intensely competitive that they drain all the fun out of it.

My heart pounding, I watch my son swing and miss. Please get a hit, I think, just this one time. Let him taste happiness and success this first time. The pitcher throws ... "Ball four!" I hear. Elation mixes with relief. But wait: It's not over yet. The umpire summons me to the mound to pitch. At this level of competition, after two walks in an inning, the coach must pitch to his own player until he strikes out or gets a hit.

What cruel fate is this? I walk slowly to the mound, acutely aware of the eyes on me. Those of my son. My wife. The other players and parents. This, I think, is the classic no-win situation.

I swallow and close my eyes. Reopened, they see my son looking back at me, expressionless. He is crouched at the plate. This is just like we've done hundreds of times in practice, I want to remind him. It'll be nice and easy; all you have to do is just hit the ball. I throw. He swings. "Strike three!" I hear, and echoes from the past resound in my ears. I hurry off the mound to console my son. "Sorry, big guy," I say. He doesn't answer. "That was a good swing," I add lamely. He simply takes his seat on the bench. He won't look my way, but he's rubbing at his eyes. I can't bear to search out my wife in the crowd; this will be a cold, quiet night at home, I think. I wonder if I'll be sleeping on the couch tonight.

But sports, like life, keeps moving on. My son had wanted to be a pitcher, the star of the show, the center of attention. Why not second base, I countered. But he was adamant. I want to pitch, he insisted. So we worked at it. Most of last summer, he pitched, I caught. Most of the spring, he pitched and I caught. My knees hurt, my back ached, and my hand stung. But he worked and he worked.

I, too, had wanted to be a pitcher when I was his age. Instead, I played right field. The part of the field where no one hit the ball. I never even had the chance to succeed or fail in the field. In truth, I wasn't as good as my friends who could catch a fly ball on the run, or effortlessly glove a grounder and rifle a throw to first. Certainly I could never fire a ball over the plate with sweet precision. Could my son? Could he succeed, or would he fail? And how would that affect him?

"Okay, son, you're pitching this inning," I hear myself saying. "Just stay relaxed, and throw it over the plate." He nods and trots to the mound. "Hey!" I call after him. He looks over at me, his face grim. "Have some fun, okay?"

I pace the dugout. If I'm this nervous, what must he be feeling? I ache for him, helpless to ease his fears. I hear the crowd calling out his name in encouragement. Pretty heady stuff for a 9-year-old, I think. Can I watch this? Can I handle this? Can he?

He's finished warming up. The batter steps in. My son stares in, concentrating, focusing on the moment. He toes the rubber, goes into his windup, and lets fly. "Strike one!" I hear. A rush of momentary elation. A good start. "Strike two!" the ump shouts out. "Wow," I hear someone say, "that kid's got some zip on the ball." Yeah, yeah, the eternal pessimist in me thinks, but it's only two strikes.

He winds up and throws again. "Strike three!" I hear, and the fans are cheering. The team is hollering at him, and so am I. He strides around the mound like a king in his throne room. Bring on the next victim. Off with his head.

Zip, zip, zip. He's in a groove, throwing bullets. He is overpowering, and the batters are helpless against this onslaught. He sets the second batter down on a called third strike, but runs the count full on the third batter. C'mon, I mutter, you can do it. Just throw a strike. I hold my breath as he winds up. He lets loose, the ball spins through the air as if in slow motion, and memories fly through my head in the fleeting moment before the ball plops into the catcher's mitt. "Strike three!" I hear. He has struck out the side.

I look out at my first-born. He pumps his fist and a huge grin splits his face as he trots off the mound.

He's not nervous, I think. He's not afraid. He's having the time of his life.

And so, I realize, am I.

29 - It's All In How You Play The Game

"Strike one!"

My son grimaces as the umpire gleefully miscalls a pitch that is a good foot outside the plate.

I sigh. Such is life in Little League baseball. Grumbling is heard from the team's parental supporters. But so far it is polite grumbling: "How could that ump call that a strike?" says one parent. "He could at least be consistent," allows another spectator.

"Ball one!" the ump hollers out. Now come the groans from the other side. "That was right over the plate, ump!" "Hey, what do you have to do to get a strike called?"

The answer is on the next pitch. "Strike two!"

Now the grumbling intensifies. The comments become a bit more pointed: "Jeez, call them the same for both teams, ump." The kids join in, moaning and groaning about the officiating. "Man, no way was that a strike," I hear one player say. "Yeah, this ump is terrible," says another.

I agree. I would join in the cascade of catcalls, but I'm feeling too lazy in the warm sunshine. I close my eyes. The hum of the game recedes. My thoughts drift …

My son loves sports, as do I. He follows big league baseball, basketball, football, even hockey with a passion. He has learned so much from sports: The value of teamwork, of discipline, hard work, sacrifice. He idolizes many professional sports figures. They serve as his role models and …

There is a commotion on the field. It all appears hazy to me, as in a dream. It seems my son has struck out. Oh, my; he is screaming at the ump in disbelief. The coach is running out onto the field, getting in the face of the ump, and now they are screaming at each other. I look around the stands; parents are on their feet screaming at the ump, the coach, the players, each other.

Play resumes. The next batter comes up. He has a huge wad of chewing gum in his mouth. At least I hope it's chewing gum. He taps his bat on home plate and spits. Eww. How disgusting. He reaches down and grabs his crotch. Oh dear. I glance surreptitiously at the boy's mother; surely she is mortified with embarrassment. No, she is yelling something about killing the ball. I hope it's the ball she's talking about.

Back to the batter. He watches a called strike slide by in disdain. He steps out of the batter's box, hawks up another huge glob, grabs his crotch again, and ambles back to the plate. What's with this constant re-arrangement of body parts, I wonder. Where does this kid get the idea that the average sports fan wants to see such personal business conducted so publicly?

He finishes his reorganization and glares at the pitcher. The pitcher glares back. Putting on their game faces, they call it. Let your opponent know you hate his guts, even if he is a year or two shy of being a teen-ager.

The pitch is inside. The batter takes a menacing step toward the mound, raising his bat like a club. The pitcher throws his glove down and raises his fists. The umpire steps between them, and settles them down. Gee, I think, this is just like the big leagues.

The batter lines the next pitch into left field. He stops at second, but his mouth starts up. "Hey, pitcher, you ain't got nothing. You can't get the ball by me." And more of the same, until he ends with the worst of all insults for a 12-year-old: "Hey, pitcher, you throw like a girl!"

Hmmm, I wonder, what happened to congratulating your opponent for making a good play? What happened to respecting your opponents?

Another hit. The trash talker rounds third and heads home. The throw is late, and he barrels into the catcher, knocking him backward about five feet. He jumps up and whoops. He turns to the catcher sprawled in the dirt. Good, I think, he's going to see if he's OK and help him up. But, no, he's standing over him, jeering and taunting him. Then he struts back to the dugout where he is roundly congratulated for his fine play.

Another hit. There's a close play at first. The throw is on time, but in the dirt, and I see the first baseman clearly drop the ball. He scoops it up late. "He's out! He's out!" he yells to the umpire, showing him the ball in the glove. The ump was screened from the play and hesitates before calling the runner out. The first baseman grins smugly, knowing he has conned the ump.

What happened, I wonder, to honesty? Shouldn't he tell the umpire that he really dropped the ball?

The runner, meanwhile, is giving the umpire an earful. Jeez, I think, since when did kids start acting like, well, overpaid professional athletes who whine about every play?

His coach is now screaming at the ump, too. The other coach, not wanting to be outdone, runs out onto the field and joins in. Both are yelling to beat the band. I'm wondering how long this game will last at this rate. My ears are starting to hurt, too.

The coach comes back to the dugout closest to us. I hear him muttering to his team about the umpires. "Gotta keep leaning on them, guys," he explains. "Gotta keep up the pressure, or else we won't get the calls. We gotta get every edge."

Ah, I think. So that's it. All this is about competitiveness. We're teaching our kids how to be competitive. Do whatever it takes to win. Belittle your opponents, bully your teammates, bluff the officials, get ahead, stay ahead, kick them when they're down. That's what we're teaching our kids: Basic, twenty-first century sportsmanship.

"Strike three!"

I am jolted from my reverie. I look around sheepishly. I've been daydreaming. Or maybe daymaring; my idle thoughts certainly were nightmarish.

Back to reality. I look out on the field. My son has just struck out. I jump to my feet in dismay. The pitch was nowhere near the plate. He's walking back to the dugout, shaking his head. His face, however, is not twisted into a snarling grimace, but a rueful grin. He knows it was a bad call, and he's chuckling about it.

I, however, fail to see the humor of the situation.

"Hey!" I yell out, glaring at the ump.

I pause. I ponder.

"Nice try, son," I hear myself saying. "You did well. Real well."

30 - Taking Back Your Telephone

There are a lot of advantages to working at home – my dog, for instance, isn't constantly carping about the office dress code – but one disadvantage is that you don't have a chance to talk to a lot of people.

Except for the telemarketers, of course.

It's actually kind of interesting to consider the types of things people try to sell over the telephone. I mean, who would ever have thought that you could sell septic tanks by phone? Which came first, do you suppose, the idea to sell something - anything - by phone or the need to boost sales of septic systems? Was the board of some septic tank corporation glumly plotting how sales were going down the drain and some bright-eyed young account executive saved the day by suggesting that, hey, why don't we just call everybody on the planet and see if they would like to buy our product?

These are the types of questions that pop into your mind when the phone rings to interrupt you while you are doing important work in your office at home, such as clipping your fingernails. Often, I admit, I am annoyed by these intrusions. But there are times when I don't mind, too much, since it is contact with the outside world, and sometimes I am feeling downright sociable. Even when the call is not necessarily flattering.

"Hello," I say, picking up the phone.

"Hello," the voice says back to me. "As a senior citizen, you are eligible to sign up…"

"Excuse me," I break in. "I hate to interrupt your pitch, but I'm not a senior citizen."

"You're not?" The voice sounds surprised.

"No," I apologize. "I'm terribly sorry."

"Oh. I see. There must be some mistake, then."

"That's all right. You can finish your spiel if you'd like," I say encouragingly.

"No, I don't think so. You don't qualify. You have to be 65. Or older."

"What is it that I don't qualify for?"

"I'm sorry, I don't think I'm authorized to disclose that information to someone who doesn't qualify. You just admitted that you're not 65."

"Well, how about if you pretend I'm 65?"

"No. I don't think that would be allowed."

"How about if you hang up and call me back and we just start over? I won't tell you that I'm not 65. Would that work?"

"I'd have to check with my supervisor. Look, I'm going to have to hang up now, OK?"

"Say," I say. "I've got an idea. Why don't you give me your number and I'll call you? How about dinner time?"

Talking to a dial tone is annoying, so I try not to be rude to telemarketers and simply hang up on them. I think politeness is appropriate even with salespeople. And I think that people forget that just because someone is trying to sell them something over the telephone that their only choices are to be extremely rude or exceedingly gullible. I think there is room for some middle ground, particularly with telemarketers who, let's face it, were probably talking on the telephone when the line formed to pass out the brains.

I got a call recently that began, "Is this Smith Timothy?"

"Yes," I agreed cautiously.

There was a puzzled pause. "Is your first name 'Smith'?"

I considered this. "No," I finally answered. "That would be my last name." Then, to be helpful, I added, "Perhaps you don't see the comma. You know, 'Smith comma Timothy,' which means last name first, then first name last."

"Ah." Another pause. "Well, Mr. Tim ... um, Smith, I am with the National Football League and..."

"No kidding?" I say, thinking, well, that explains a lot. "So, what position do you play?"

"Er, position? I don't play a position, I'm..."

"Oh. So you're like, what, a coach? Or a whaddayacallit, a scout? Is this about my son? Because if it is, he's only 14, and I have to tell you I think that's too young to be recruited. Besides, he hasn't really played much football. But since you're asking, how much money are we talking here?"

"Money? I don't ... what money?"

"You know. The signing bonus. How much? We need to be talking seven figures, I have to be honest with you on this, if he's going to go right from the ninth grade to the pros, you know."

"Sir, I think there's been a misunderstanding. I'm not calling to recruit your son. This is about a credit card."

"A credit card? Are you out of your mind? I just told you, he's only 14. Great galloping ghosts, man, do you realize what a 14-year-old would do with a credit card? Do you have any idea how much those video games cost?"

"No, no, no. Sir. The card is not for your son. It's for you."

"Oh," I say. "Geez, why didn't you say so up front, without going off on a tangent like that?"

"Sir, we would like to offer you a credit card in your favorite team's colors and with its logo. We…"

"Really? Say, that's a swell idea. Did you think of that? They should give you a raise. Hmmm, let me think a minute. My favorite team, huh? I guess I'll go with the Hornets, then."

"The Hornets? Sir, I don't think there is a NFL team named the Hornets."

"There's not? Are you sure? I'm pretty sure it's some kind of insect. Can you check?"

"I'm quite sure, sir. I believe the Hornets are an NBA team. They play basketball."

"You might be right about that. That's the one with the round ball, right? And your guys play with what, that oblong kind of pointy ball, right?"

"Correct, sir."

"I gotcha. OK, then, how about we go with the Tar Heels, then? They play football, don't they?"

"Yes, sir, they do, but that is a college team. They're not pros."

"There's a difference? Well, let's see. Hmmm, so do you have, like, a list of these teams of yours? Could you read some of the teams out to me?"

"A list? Well, yes. Here you go: Arizona, Baltimore, Cincinnati, Cleveland…"

"That's it. Cleveland. I'll take Cleveland."

"The Browns?"

"Yeah. Say, does that mean the credit card is going to be brown?"

"Er, that is one of the team's colors, sir. Brown and orange."

"Brown and orange? Who wants a brown and orange credit card? It'll look like I dropped it in the mud. I can just see all these cashiers in all these stores trying to wipe the non-existent mud off my credit card before they swipe it. Besides, I thought they were the Reds."

"The Reds? No, sir, that would be Cincinnati. Only that's their baseball team. Their football team is called the Bengals."

"You mean like tigers? They have a lot of them in southern Ohio, do they?"

"I wouldn't know, sir. I think only in the zoo…"

"So why do you suppose they didn't pick some other zoo animal? Like camels. That at least is alliterative. You know, Cincinnati Camels. It kind of has a nice ring to it, don't you think?"

"I wouldn't know, sir. I…"

"Getting back to the Browns. Do you have some other colors?"

"Absolutely. Minnesota, for instance is purple…"

"No. I mean as their name. You know, like is there a Pittsburgh Pinks or a Miami Mauve, for instance?"

"I don't think so, sir. You know, perhaps there's been a mistake. I think I've called the wrong number."

"Does that mean I don't get to choose a team?"

"Not only do you not get a team, sir, we're flagging this number."

"Is that like a penalty? Backfield in motion, that sort of thing?"

"It means your phone number will be red-flagged for all telemarketers, warning them not to call."

"Aw, gee, really? And just when I was thinking about buying a new septic tank, too."

31 - It's Time For A Vacation

"Well, family," I say, "where shall we go on vacation this year?"

"Anywhere but to my office," my wife promptly replies.

"To a baseball game," my son suggests.

"Shopping!" my daughter pipes up.

I sigh. "Let me try to explain," I try to explain. "This is our one chance all year to do something really fun. Something bigger than games and shopping. Something we will all remember."

"How about the beach?" my son says.

"The beach. That's good. Now we're talking. Surf, sand, and sun."

"Heat, humidity, and hassle," my wife mutters.

"What was that?" I ask.

"Nothing," she smiles sweetly.

"We can do the beach," I agree, "but I was thinking about something a bit more ambitious. Like taking a long train ride and going out West."

"Will it be like Tweetsie?" my daughter wants to know.

"Sort of. Only this train goes faster. And it's bigger. And you can sleep on it."

"Will we see cowboys and Indians?"

"Perhaps. Only today they're called Native Americans and cowpersons, er, cow, um, mobile bovine engineering specialists."

"You're making this up, aren't you Dad?"

"Of course not. So, how does that sound?"

"Cool," my son says. "Can I take my video games?"

I frown, as though I'm actually giving this notion serious thought. "I think not."

"Boy, some vacation this will be." He crosses his arms in a huff.

"Does this mean I'll miss my TV shows?" my daughter asks, lower lip trembling.

I try to break it to her gently. "Yes."

She starts sobbing.

"I'm sorry, sweetie," I console her. "It's just that they don't have television sets west of the Mississippi. Don't they teach you these things in school?"

She's weeping uncontrollably now.

I sigh. I look at my wife. "You know," I say accusingly, "it was your idea to have kids. It was my idea for the two of us to go on a cruise alone every year."

As always, she easily parries this cutting verbal attack. "I have to go to work," she says.

"Dad?" my daughter coughs out between sobs. "Do we have to go on vacation?"

Time, I realize, for a little fatherly chat to explain how things work in the real world. "Look, kids, watching TV and playing video games is not all there is to life. It's time to go out and see things. Do things. Travel and experience different stuff."

I can see my argument is unconvincing, so I try a different tack. "Besides, it's kind of like a law that we have to take a vacation every year."

"It is?" my daughter asks.

"Yeah, right," my son sneers.

"No, no, really. It's the American way to get out and see this country of ours. We're supposed to help out the national economy by spreading our money around in different places. It's downright un-American to sit around and do nothing at home when you should be out traveling. So let's start planning this trip."

Easier said than done. Modern travel planning can be accomplished either through specialists, who plot your itinerary and arrange for ticketing based on professional expertise, or on your own through the wonders of the Internet. Being of the male persuasion, I naturally choose to head off into the cyberwilds on my own.

I discover all sorts of amazing things as I explore the realm of on-line travel planning. Such as the fact that airline tickets prices are pegged not to any logical standard, such as, oh, actual distance flown, but to some obscure formula that is far too complex to get into now but has to do with flight vectors, hub rotation patterns, directional frequency zones and Oriental beverage prices. Suffice to say that it is cheaper to fly to Honolulu from Baltimore on Wednesdays in July (excluding leap years) than it is to park your car in the long-term lot for a week.

Airline ticket pricing actually has much in common with the stock market: Up one day, down the next. Prices quoted one day are history the next.

I also noticed that several ticket prices I checked seemed to be misquotes. My only recourse was to call the airline and have them clarify matters.

"Yes, I was trying to purchase a ticket on your airline over the Internet and noticed a mistake in your prices. I need a one-way ticket and it says here that it costs half-again as much as a round-trip ticket. Isn't that backward?" I chuckle to show them that I'm being a good sport about their typos.

"That would be correct, sir."

"What would be?"

"The price, sir."

"You're telling me you charge more to fly to a city than to fly there and back?"

"That is correct, sir."

"Don't you find that a bit odd?"

"Odd?"

"Yes, odd. As in unusual."

"Not at all sir. It all has to do with flight vectors…"

"Yes, yes. But see here, I also notice that this same round-trip flight is cheaper if I fly here from there and then back than if I fly from here to there first and then back."

"Your point being, sir?"

"Can I buy the there-to-here-and-back-again ticket and not use the first half but just use the second part?"

"I wouldn't advise it, sir."

"You wouldn't?"

"Not if you expect us not to cancel the return portion of a ticket you didn't use."

"You would cancel it?"

"Not me personally, sir, but yes, this airline would."

"Isn't that illegal?"

"How droll, sir. I suppose your contributions to Congress exceeded that of the airline industry for the past fiscal year?"

"So I'm just supposed to take what you give me?"

"That's the ticket. Oh, and by the way, don't forget to apply for those frequent flyer miles."

"Um, how do I do that?"

"Oh, many credit cards give you points toward frequent flyer miles. You can get all sorts of free trips."

"I can?"

"Absolutely. For instance, if you were to buy a $100,000 house using a credit card, you would earn enough points to, let's see, fly free to Godthab anytime between January and February."

"Godthab? Where the heck is that?"

"Geographically challenged, are we sir? That would be in Greenland. West coast."

"How many miles would I get if I purchased your round-trip ripoff we discussed earlier?"

"I think we could manage a free bus shuttle from the airport parking lot of your choice."

And so it went. Week after week of browsing for airline deals, train tickets, inexpensive hotels, rent-a-car specials. But at last all the arrangements are made, tickets bought, reservations made, confirmations received. Finally, I break the joyous news to the family that we're all set and it's time to pack the bags.

"That's great, Dad," say my kids, breaking their gaze away from the TV. "But the summer's almost over. It's about time to go back to school."

"What? Huh?" I babble, bleary eyed from computer glare. I look at the calendar. Sheeez, time sure flies. I realize suddenly that I'm exhausted.

Boy, do I need a vacation.

32 - Getting Away From It All

Vacation: *n.* A period of time devoted to pleasure, rest, or relaxation. A holiday.

We're on the road, car packed to the roof, roaring down the interstate. Gosh, what a wonderful highway system we have here in America: You can drive 75 mph and still not see anything more exciting than the occasional road kill for the better part of a week.

I notice that other drivers seem to ease the boredom by talking on their cellular phones. I wonder to whom they could be talking. After all, I have a phone right here; who would I call? What would I say? "Hey, I thought I'd call and tell you I'm driving down the interstate near, let's see, East Greaselick. How ya doin'?" I mean, who would want to get a phone call like that?

But that is just idle contemplation. Right now I'm relaxed, rested, away from the stress and struggle of everyday workaday life. Even if I am rushing along in bumper-to-bumper traffic at such high rates of speed that one momentary lapse of concentration could mean...

"Kids!" I yell, whirling around to face them in the back of the car, my concentration on driving momentarily lapsing. "Stop that bickering right now or I'll turn around and go home."

"But, Dad," my son says smugly. "You can't turn around on an interstate. There's no exit here."

Kids. What are they teaching them in school these days?

Finally, it's time to stop for the night. We find a nice motel and pull in.

"Does it have a pool?" the kids ask at once. "Don't stop if it doesn't have a pool, Dad."

"Not to worry kids. There's the pool. And look, there's not a soul in it. You'll have it all to yourselves."

We check in. We find our room. We unload our stuff. The kids make a beeline for the pool. Ah, I think: Now, this is restful. This is relaxing. This is vacation.

The kids return. My daughter is sobbing. "Dad, the pool's closed!"

"What do you mean? It's early yet. Surely they haven't closed it." I march down to the pool. There is a sign on the gate.

"POOL CLOSED for stabilization. Will reopen tomorrow." I sigh. How the heck do you stabilize a pool? I wonder. And what happened to it that it now requires stabilization?

"Sorry, kids," I say, "We'll just have to make do."

"Daddy," my daughter says, still fighting back tears. "Can we go to the toy store instead then?"

"Sweetie, I don't think there are any toy stores near here."

"Yes there is. Across the street. See, over there."

She points. I look.

"Um, sweetie, I don't think they have the kind of toys we'd be interested in."

"But Dad, it says 'TOYS' in big letters. And there's stuff for big people, too, because it says 'ADULT' on the sign."

I hustle her back in the room. "Let's go eat!" I say.

Back on the road. Zooming along, I wonder why it is that turn signals are no longer used. Have they deleted the "Proper Use of the Turn Signal" chapter from driver's education courses? Do people not get curious when buying a car and ask the salesman, "Say, by the way, what is this stick attached to the steering wheel for anyway?"

And another thing: Where in the driver's manual does it tell you that when you pass someone to immediately slow down as soon as you pull back in front of them in their lane?

But enough griping. This is a vacation. A rest stop is coming up. We've made a picnic lunch; a little fresh air, a chance to stretch our legs … it will be restful and relaxing. We pull in. We pile out.

"Whew," I gasp. "This fresh air is kind of warm, isn't it?" It feels like a furnace; the heat rolls off the pavement in waves. Sweat is already trickling down my face as I lug lunch over to a picnic table. As we eat, I notice there are a lot of people wandering around talking on their cell phones. I try not to imagine what kind of conversations they are having, but it does no good. "Marge, we're here at a rest stop. Nice place. They have bathrooms and everything. Yep, already went."

The people at the next picnic table over aren't talking on a phone, but they are talking to their dog. It's one of those little yappy things that you're always afraid of stepping on. "Oops! Was that your pet? Sorry. Say, you don't have something I can scrape this stuff off my shoe with, do you?"

Anyway, they're putting this dog up on top of the picnic table. Now they're putting food out for it to eat.

"Ewwww," my kids say.

"Ewwww," I think, looking at the top of our picnic table, wondering what's been on it recently. "Time to hit the road," I say.

Miles and miles and miles we go. My, isn't this fun. Not to say restful and relaxing.

Ah, the beach at last. We pull into a motel. There's the pool. There are people in it. The kids are excited. I am relieved. I grin at my wife.

"Dear," she says, "I think it's beginning to rain."

I laugh. I squint at the sky. It does look dark and threatening. "It's OK," I say, "even if it does rain, it will only be a few drops. Then it will pass over."

We check in. As we head back to the car, I notice it is pouring outside.

"Wow," says the desk clerk. "We haven't had a drop of rain here in three months."

"Really?" I say.

"Yeah, but don't worry," he says. "It's just a shower. It will pass over."

The kids want to know why they can't go in the pool in the rain since, after all, wet is wet. I explain about lightning and its subtle yet potentially distressing effects on things soaking in small bodies of water.

"But don't worry," I tell them confidently. "These showers pass quickly."

Hours later as we prepare for bed, the rain thundering down outside, I reassure them that the storm will pass and we'll be swimming tomorrow. I eye the two motel beds. "Dear," I say, "I don't think two adults can fit in one of these beds together." I look at the kids. "Hey, guys, want to camp on the floor?"

Already unhappy over the pool thing, as though I was the one who made up the rule about no swimming while lightning is striking within 15 feet, they both look at me as though to suggest that perhaps I should sleep in the car. Or the pool. I sigh. I climb into one of the alleged beds with my son while my wife gets in the other one with our daughter. As I doze off to the drumming of rain on the roof and the beating of my son's toes in my shin, I think, gee, I used to get excited about staying in a motel.

But the sun finally does shine, and the beach awaits. We pack up our beach accoutrements and head out. A large weather-beaten sign greets us. At the top is a huge "NO" followed by a long list.

"Gee," I say, "they sure have a lot of rules for a beach, don't they?"

"Dad?" my son asks. "If that sign says 'no vehicles' why is that policeman driving a four-wheeler on the beach?"

"Well, son, because the police don't have to obey … um, they get to … ah, they're patrolling, you see."

"Why?"

"Why?"

"Yeah. Why are they patrolling? What are they patrolling? Is there like a lot of crime on the beach or something?"

"Um, well, no." I think fast. "But that's because there are police out patrolling. See?"

"I guess. So are they going to come and rub suntan lotion on us?"

"I wouldn't think so. Why do you ask?"

"Because he's rubbing it on that lady's back."

"Um, I think he's just providing a special service to her. She probably has arthritis or something and can't rub it on herself."

Your tax dollars at work, I think. I wonder just what else a beach cop does. Do they shoot you if you go out too far in the water? Do they arrest you for self-endangerment if you get sunburned? I'd hate to think of the consequences if I landed in a jail cell with some oversized, deranged felon and was asked what I was in for and had to answer that I was framed and the cops had planted that glass container on me at the beach.

Despite these thoughts, I love the beach. There's something about the sun and sea and sand that lulls the senses. This, I think, is the stereotypical vacation spot. It just doesn't get any better than this. That's probably exactly what all those people out in the waves are saying as they talk on their cell phones, I muse.

Of course, vacations aren't all just a day at the beach. There is your obligatory shopping for souvenirs to be done to reassure you that you've actually been somewhere, there's your visiting all the local scenic and historic spots, there's your standing in line to partake of the local entertainment which usually involves windmills and giant plaster giraffes, and of course there's your search for somewhere to sit down and enjoy a soothing libation.

Ah, there's nothing like a nice cold margarita to take the edge off the heat. I can't wait to slurp this one down...

"Excuse me, um, miss? Could I get some ice in my drink?"

The waitress looks at me blankly.

"Ice?" I repeat. I point at my wife's drink. "Like hers. You know, with ice. Cold." I clutch my arms and shiver to mime cold, even though it's 98 degrees in this "open air" establishment.

She looks at me, clearly uncomprehending. It dawns on me that she has just gotten off the boat from Sweden or wherever, someplace where they don't need ice in their drinks.

"How about a glass of ice? Could you bring me a glass of ice, please?"

"Dear," me wife says, "she's not deaf. You don't have to raise your voice."

"I'm not raising my voice," I say loudly. "I'm enunciating so that she can understand me, because she clearly does not speak the English language."

The transplanted Scandinavian brings me a glass of ice. I pour my warm green drink into it. Now I have a margarita on the rocks. The salt that goes with it, or course, is on the rim of the now-empty glass. I lick one glass and sip the other. It's a bit like rubbing your stomach while patting your head. But, hey, it's OK, because I'm on vacation. I'm resting and relaxing.

"Honey, you look tense. Are you all right?" Yes, I'm all right. I can handle petty annoyances because it's a vacation. You're supposed to be having fun and, by golly, you're going to have fun no matter what. You're on holiday, dammit.

Of course, a body can take only so much relaxation, so when the vacation ends you're sad it's over, but happy to be going home. And won't it be great to be home. Your own bed: Yes! It sleeps two comfortably! Your own stuff. Your own food. And, most importantly, your own bathroom.

"Ah," I say to my family as we relax after our vacation. "Isn't this great? No matter where you go or what you do, there's just no place better than home."

"Dad?" my daughter asks.

"Hmmm?"

"So where are we going next year?"

Part V

Getting Older

33 - *Home Work*

It's a beautiful day to go to the office. Particularly when your office is right upstairs.

Ah, the joys of working out of your own home. Modern technology and bottom-line practicality wed to produce a low-cost, high-tech, work-at-home telecommuting labor force. What a boost for employee morale: The only rush hour traffic to combat is in the kitchen at breakfast. Button-down shirts and oxygen-starving ties, makeup and hose and heels - they all gather dust in lieu of what's fashionable for any season around the house: baggy sweat shirts and loose jeans and dirty sneakers. Bad hair day? Ha! It's who cares day. And the only jockeying for position at this office is the settling down of your buns on the chair just right.

Yes, working at home is the best of all possible worlds. Less formality. Greater freedom. More flexibility. Higher productivity and lower stress. And, of course, it provides much, much more time to spend with the kids. Play time. Educational time. Important time. Quality time. They're growing up fast, you know, and you don't want to miss out on any of those precious moments of youth.

Such as when you're trying to work. The kids are out of school for a couple of days? Not a problem. Work around them. It'll be fine. They'll be good. They'll behave. This will work.

Let's start them off with the old reliable. It's not exactly the most politically correct baby-sitter, but, hey, what's wrong with a little TV? All right, kids, you watch some cartoons while I do a little work. OK?

Let's see, I need to get down to work. Here we go.

"Dad?"

"Yes?" A model of politeness and concern. It's important to take the time to communicate with your children when they need something. It might be important advice they seek, or some gap in their knowledge they thirst to fill, or simply a moment to tap that vast store of parental wisdom.

"Can I have something to eat?"

"But we just had breakfast a few minutes ago."

"I know, but I'm still hungry."

"We'll have a snack in a little while, OK?" Hoping the child doesn't see the half of donut perched next to the coffee cup.

Back to work. Gosh, it's noisy. "Hey, kids, turn that TV down a little, will you?" Jeez, the thing must be turned all the way up. Now, where was I?

"Dad?"

"Yes, son, what is it?" Careful, keep that edge of impatience out of your voice. It's important to hear your children out, to allow them to express themselves fully, to communicate across the generations.

"I'm bored."

"Bored? How can you be bored? Why don't you go outside? It's a beautiful day. Go outside and play."

"OK. Dad?"

"Yes, son?"

"Do you know where my shoes are?"

"No, son, I do not." Was that just a hint of exasperation creeping into my voice? "I'm not in charge of keeping up with shoes." That's your mother's job, I say to myself.

Back to work. I hear a ball bouncing outside. Hmmm. A little pickup game with the kids would be much better than work. No. Not now. Work first, play later. Let's keep our priorities straight.

"Dad?"

"Yes, what is it?" Careful, that was definitely more than a hint of exasperation. More like a touch of irritation.

"Is it lunch time yet?"

"No, not yet."

"When will it be?"

"Soon. Why don't you go outside and play with your brother for awhile? I need to finish up a few things." You mean start a few things, I say to myself.

Whew. All right, let's have at it. Work, work, work. What's all that shouting?

"Hey, kids, what's going on?"

"He hit me with the ball!"

"Did not!"

"Did too! On my arm. See, Dad?"

"Look, you guys, I'm trying to work here, OK? So work out your problems. Or play by yourselves for awhile if you can't get along today."

Gee whiz. Can't a person get any peace and quiet anymore? Now, where was I?

"Dad?"

"WHAT?" Oops, calm yourself. Don't yell at the kids. They just want to be involved in your life. "What?"

"We're hungry."

A sigh. Surrender. "OK. Fine. Go have a snack. But, please, kids, leave me alone for just a little while, OK?" Don't whine, I tell myself, it sets a bad example.

"Sure, Dad. We promise."

Now, then, great, let's just do it, as they say. Let's tackle this work stuff and get it done. Oh, great, look at them out there.

"Hey, kids, what are you doing? When I said you could have a snack I didn't mean ice cream!"

"Why not?"

"Because it's still morning, that's why."

"So?"

"So ... It's a law that you can't eat ice cream in the morning," I lie with practiced parental smoothness. "Everybody knows that." Besides, your mother would skin us all alive if she found out.

"Sorry, Dad."

"It's OK. Just don't do it again."

"Sure."

All right, I'm really going to work now. I have to get at this stuff. Focus. Concentrate.

"Um, Dad?"

"WHATWHATWHATWHATWHAT?!" The heck with calm and collected. We've passed exasperation, sailed by irritation, and gone directly to foaming-at-the-mouth frustration. "Enough with the 50 questions. How many more questions must I answer today? Every two minutes, it's another question. I don't have any more answers, understand? No more questions, got it? Now, can you just leave me alone for a few minutes?"

"Gosh, Dad, I was just going to see if you wanted to play with us." There's that hang dog expression, calculated to extract the maximum amount of guilt. Well, I'm not falling for any of that.

"I would love to play with you guys. But you know what? I have to work. So let me work right now. Then we'll play. Don't you have any work to do? What about that school project you're supposed to be working on? Why don't you work on that?"

"OK."

"Well? Why are you just standing there?"

"If I'm going to work on my project I need to use the computer."

I stare at my first-born child. Suddenly I'm thinking about an office. With four walls and a door. That closes. I'm thinking about an office with a desk that doesn't have any toys on it. An office filled with adults, with nary a child in sight. A place where people talk about adult things, like politics, world affairs, sports. Where people with real problems and real concerns and real troubles come and go every day, a place bustling with activity. A place that pays you to be there day after day, acting like an adult.

I look at my son. I look at my daughter. I look at my office.

"Kids," I say slowly, "this is a beautiful day. Let's go play."

34 - In The Waiting Room

I arrive early, since my mother taught me to be punctual.

It will be a few minutes before the doctor will see you, I am told.

Fine. No problem. I am a patient person. Besides, today I have a bona fide appointment, made weeks in advance. None of this work-you-in-when-we-can stuff.

I'll just make myself comfortable over here.

This is great. This will give me a couple of minutes to relax, to escape the hustle and bustle of the real world, to contemplate and reflect on the truly important things in life...

I look at my watch. Five minutes have elapsed. Enough of this reflection stuff. I am weak with boredom.

I get up and browse through the brochures. Perhaps I'll pick up a few tips for healthy living. Here's one: "Two Steps Toward Better Health." I open it up. Step. 1: "Don't eat anything with any taste." Step 2: "Don't do anything that's any fun."

Gee. Now those are words to live by, I think. But what kind of life would it be?

I look at another. "Stop Smoking Now!" it says. "Smoking" is in big red letters, signifying fire, I suppose. Or danger. Ah. I see it's really an ad for one of those patches. I snicker: Those things never work. Hmmm. This one says to place a patch over the mouth for six weeks. That just might work, I admit.

I shift in my seat. They really should have a brochure on what to do for buttitis, I think.

I try the magazines. Here's one with a cover story about the election. I shake my head. Surely Reagan isn't running again?

I give up on reading. I survey the waiting room. It is nearly full, almost all the seats taken. With sick people, I suddenly realize. People a lot sicker than I want to be. Diseased people. Who knows what kinds of germs are lurking about in here, just waiting to pounce?

Somebody coughs. Oh, great, I think. Like my doctor's going to admit I caught tuberculosis in his waiting room. I try not to breathe.

The day is passing by. I grow wearier by the minute. If I'm here much longer, I'll want to get on his pension plan.

I'm also beginning to wonder if this mandatory 45-minute waiting period before you can see your doctor imposed by Congress is such a good idea.

At last! My name is called. Oh, was ever there a sweeter sound heard?

I bound up from my seat. This is it! Entry into the inner sanctum, away from the poor dreary souls left to wait out the day in a dull stupor. Hah!

I go down the hall and we stop at the scales to be weighed. Hop up? No, wait! I can't weigh that much. Let me take off my shoes. Let me take off my ... here, just a minute. Too late. I am led into an examining room.

Very nice. Interesting wallpaper. What a nice still life of a bowl of fruit. You don't see art like that in galleries anymore.

I fidget. There are more magazines, but I resist the urge to read all about the 1988 Olympics. Besides, there are all kinds of strange looking instruments cluttering up the room, clearly designed for some unimaginable medical purposes.

I hear a coffee pot somewhere down the hall wheezing and gasping, sounding for all the world like some sort of artificial lung machine.

At least I hope it's a coffee maker.

Something somewhere dings. Perhaps a microwave oven? What on earth could they be cooking out there? I don't want to carry that thought any further. Now I hear a muffled clatter. I look at the equipment in my tiny room and wonder what kinds of noise they make - or cause you to make.

I am definitely getting antsy. At least that is my diagnosis. What's happening out there? What's going on? Where is everyone? What are they doing? And when are they going to do it to me?

The doctor breezes in, startling me out of my reverie. A nurse takes my blood pressure. A little high, you say? Imagine that.

So, what seems to be the problem, I am asked.

Good question. I was kind of hoping that whichever one of us had gone to medical school might answer that.

The poking and prodding and probing begin. Does this hurt? You bet. Hey, and stay away from that thing on the wall, OK?

At last the diagnosis is made. The prescription is prescribed. The bill is presented.

Ouch. Now, *that* hurt.

But now I get to leave. I exit through the still-full waiting room.

Boy, am I glad it's not me who has to see all these grumpy sick people and hear them moan and groan about what ails them. What a job.

I walk out into the world feeling better already.

35 – What Time Is It?

Time waits for no man, the saying goes – unless you're on daylight savings time.

I have to admit that the older I get, the harder it becomes to keep up with time. Especially when they up and change it on you.

As the years pass, I have an increasingly difficult time adjusting to Daylight Savings Time in the spring and the reversion back to Standard Time in the fall. It doesn't help that my clocks persist in featuring different times, possibly because I don't seem to have the technical expertise to change half of them.

Consider the clocks they put in automobiles. I push and pull various buttons and knobs while I'm trying not to run off the road, but nothing happens except I'm suddenly exiled to the realm of AM radio with no logical means to return.

And I don't dare try to reset the time on my VCR, which has flashed "12:00" since I took it out of the box. But what good would it do to set the time on it anyway if they're going to go and arbitrarily change the time a couple of times a year?

And say you've actually figured out how to set the time on your VCR and moved on to setting the timer for late-night recording. What do you do on the night the time changes? If you're taping a movie that starts at 1 a.m. and the time changes at 2 a.m., what time will it be when the movie ends? What time do you set the VCR to stop? When you gain an hour, does the movie run long, and when you lose an hour are whole reels cut from the film?

Call me old-fashioned, but I always figured that time was a constant, marching inexorably forward, pausing for no one in its relentless journey down the path of infinity. So how come it's semi-annually jerked around simply as a matter of convenience?

It should come as no surprise that time tinkering can be traced to Congress. And that should give us all pause; there's no telling what politicians will do once they've started shifting time around.

Why not move the clock back, say, every Sunday night? That way we could all gain an extra hour every week. So what if eventually we have midnight in the middle of the day; is that so different than suddenly having it get dark before you get home from work?

And who says Congress will stop at mere hours? What's to prevent them from changing whole days?

Look for time changing to become a major campaign theme, with candidates promising that, if elected, they will offer voters two Saturdays a week. Others might swear to abolish Mondays. And, of course, there would be those who promise a month of Sundays in an attempt to win over the religious right.

Pandering to special interests, candidates would promise to turn back the clocks for senior citizens, or advance time for teens to enable them to become legal adults – in exchange for their vote, naturally.

Merchants are sure to lobby Congress to move December to July and back again so that they could profit from two Christmases a year.

Since they already promise the moon, what's to prevent politicians from promising sunny days and cool nights? If time is tampered with, can the weather be far behind?

Keep in mind that what we're dealing with here are fundamental laws of nature. I think we must ask ourselves in all seriousness whether these are the sorts of laws we want lawyers rewriting. Will they be suspending the law of gravity next?

And don't think for a minute that the government has given up on the metric system yet, either. Just when they've got us guessing what time it is, they'll be back trying to ram liters down our throats again. Give them an inch and they'll take a meter. Before you know it, you'll be driving hundreds of kilometers down the road after buying a few liters of gas, wondering what happened to the congressional ban on rainy days.

But I digress. I just don't think manipulating time is such a good idea. But if they are going to change it twice a year, can't they come up with a better system? I mean, how can something so basic be so confusing? Is it really necessary to have 24 hours in a day divided into two 12-hour intervals? Thus, we have two 2 o'clocks, necessitating us to attach some strange abbreviations, a.m. and p.m. – the meaning of which nobody, by the way, has a clue – just to clarify the time of day. And try explaining to a child why a day includes the night.

Military time – which continues with 1300 after the first 12 o'clock and on up to 2400 – is much more logical, but who knows what time 1824 is without a calculator?

Then there is the calendar system. Is this a joke or what? Can you imagine trying with a straight face to explain to some higher intelligence from another planet about our calendars?

"Er, yes, some of our monthly divisions of time have 30 days and some have, um, 31 days. Yes, that includes what we call nights. And, oh, one of our months only has, um, 28 days – no, it's not being punished, it's just one of the winter months, unless you live south of the equator, and then it's a summer one – except every fourth year, when we let it have 29 days. No, honestly, I'm not making this up."

You'd think modern civilization could do better. I don't know what we were thinking when we created this whole time business. In fact, I think it's high time we came up with a whole new system of time – one that doesn't go by quite as fast as it used to.

36 - The Class Reunion

The first thing I noticed was there were a lot of old people attending my high school reunion.

This was curious, because I don't remember most of my classmates being held back year after year, but here they were, people obviously several years older than I ever thought they would be.

Then again, I reasoned, perhaps it's the heat that ages these people so. My high school is located in a tropical zone where, on this evening, the nighttime temperatures graciously dip to a level that would pass for a warm day back home in the mountains. Many of my fellow graduates surely stayed on in the area, finding gainful employment while embracing a climate that perhaps more quickly turns the hair gray, adds wrinkles, expands waistlines and enlarges seating capacities.

Or if not the heat, it could be, as they say, the humidity.

Whatever the ages, we all looked eternally young in our senior class pictures the reunion organizers had so thoughtfully affixed to our nametags. This was so we could recall what each of us actually looked like those many years ago, and to provide our spouses a few chuckles as reward for being dragged to an event in which they knew nobody, didn't care to know anybody, and would just as soon not have to know any of them again.

Truth forces me at this juncture to confirm spousal opinion that the old pictures make the members of my class look more like a bunch of goofy kids than the too-cool-to-believe Einsteins we all knew we were at the time.

It was good to hear all the music "of the times" again, although what seemed awfully offensive to adult ears then now sounds downright melodic compared to what purports to be music today. And I was frankly amazed to see some of these oldsters out there kicking up their heels in some sort of bizarre dance routine when some of the latter was played; I decided that they must get out of the house more than I do.

Many of my classmates are parents now, although I evidently started my family a little later in life because some people have kids already in the late teens and early twenties. I do the math in my head and suppress a snicker.

Coincidentally, these weary parents looked to have suffered the most from the aging process; I wonder, as I think of my own children, is there is any correlation.

Anyway, it's good to see all the people from the good ol' days, some of whom I hadn't seen in a good couple of decades. It was certainly a time far different than the one we now live in, a time of war and peace and love, of limitless hopes and distant dreams, a time seemingly of more sharply defined passions and raging emotions, not to mention hormones.

It's ironic that these quintessential anti-establishment era graduates are now so firmly entrenched in the establishment, leading middle-class lives with middle-class worries. But this is America, after all, and we haven't so much sold out as bought in, and been incorporated into the American dream. The only shame is that so many of my generation became lawyers.

I see that the people who wore clothes their parents didn't like are still wearing clothes they shouldn't. Somehow, I find a certain perverse comfort in this continuing display of adolescent fashion sense.

I see also that the years have not all been kind to some of the cheerleaders, who are learning that their pompoms can only carry them so far before they begin to let them down. And I see that the years haven't provided any enlightenment to the class snobs who ignored so many of us way back then; even peer pressure, however, diminishes with time and I find I have peace of mind now because I can afford to ignore them, too.

What I can't afford to do anymore is stay up all night partying and reminiscing. Work and responsibility and children and real life beckon. Time is precious and fleeting. There are things to do, places to go, people to see.

Enough of looking back, I decide. It's time to look ahead.

37 - Going Crazy With The Fitness Craze

Ah, spring. The time when our thoughts turn to … what the heck we're going to look like once we peel off all the layers of clothes we've worn all winter.

The image of a beached whale comes to mind. Or, more precisely, a bleached, beached whale. All that blubber served us well through the long winter months, keeping us warm and insulated against the biting cold. But now that it's time to replace the baggy sweatpants with shorts and the big, comfortable sweaters with T-shirts, well … perhaps we laid that protective layer of blubber on a bit too thick.

There's nothing for it now but to trim the fat a bit. Slim down, and while we're at it we might as well work a few of the kinks out of our bodies. Time to face facts: The couple of times we went sledding with the kids just weren't sufficient exercise to have gotten us in shape during the winter. So our only recourse is to get serious about fitness.

Hmmm. There are a lot of ways to exercise. Which is the least troublesome? I know. Bike riding is great exercise. I'll ride a bike every day and become wonderfully fit in no time.

"C'mon, kids," I say. "Let's get our bikes and go for a ride."

"Great idea, Dad!" they enthuse, racing out the door.

This will be great, I think. Exercise. Fresh air. A little quality time with the kids. I wrestle my bike off the garage wall where it has hung for months. Uh oh.

"Hang on, guys, it looks like my tires are flat." I find the pump and hook it to the front tire. I start pumping: Up and down, up and down. "Whew," I say, trying not to pant too heavily as my kids are watching my every move. "The tire needs a lot of air." Finally it is full and I move to the rear tire. I pump and pant. I pump and huff. I pump and gasp for air.

"Gee, kids," I say, feeling a bit faint. "That kind of wore me out. I think that's enough bike riding for me for one day."

"But Dad," they complain in unison, "we haven't even ridden yet."

"Hey," I reply, a bit too defensively, "you have to take this exercise thing slow, you know." Kids. They just don't understand things from an adult perspective.

So maybe the bike riding idea isn't the best. But, say, how about the trampoline in the yard? Now there's a fun way to exercise. The kids are jumping on that thing all the time, having a ball. How hard could it be?

The kids are encouraging as I clamber aboard. "Now jump real high, Dad," they yell. "Higher."

I soar up into the air. Bounce, soar. Bounce, soar. This is fun. After the sixth bounce I'm sucking in air. Two more bounces and I'm ready to puke. I climb down. My legs are wobbly as I stagger around. I wonder if the pain in my knees will subside in a couple of days.

"Kids," I hear myself saying, "I'm going to go and bounce on the sofa now, OK?"

Seriously out of shape, would be my guess. The ol' body just ain't what it used to be, not that it was any great shakes back then either. Time for drastic action. Time for serious business. Time for a fitness center.

Centuries of evolution have transformed medieval torture chambers into modern day fitness centers. The same machines and pieces of apparatus that used to be found in all the finest castle dungeons have been updated and upgraded: That one there would be the rack on which they stretch you out, and this one must be the one where they pull your shoulders out of joint with all those weights, and that one ... well, I don't even want to try to imagine what that's used for.

I am on a tour of the chamber of horrors, and my guide - I didn't catch his name but I'm pretty sure it was Igor - is clearly quite proud of the equipment as he attempts to convince me to join the club.

"Here we have all of our exercise bikes," he says with a wave of his hand at a row of gleaming machines. "They are the latest in technology."

Curious, since I wasn't aware that bicycle technology had advanced a great deal in the past millennium, I politely inquire: "Is that why it doesn't have any, um, you know, wheels?"

"Oh, you don't need wheels for these bikes."

"You don't?"

"Oh, no, these are stationary bikes."

"You mean you ride a bike that doesn't go anywhere?" I ponder the technological advance that this represents in our society. I wonder idly if there's any money to be made in letting people sit in cars without wheels and pretend to drive. "So, um, are all these bikes, what, like hooked up to a generator so they provide power or something?"

Igor just laughs. Well, I think, at least this won't involve any tire pumps.

We move on. "These are our stair steppers," he says.

"Wait, don't tell me," I say. "These stairs don't actually go anywhere, right?" Igor looks at me as he would a slow-witted child. "I mean, why couldn't you just climb the stairs over there a few times? Wouldn't that work?"

"These machines," he informs me stiffly, "are scientifically designed to provide a maximum level of workout to specific muscle groups and to improve your cardiovascular system. A simple set of stairs can't do that. Shall we move on? Over here is a rowing machine ... oh, never mind."

"What's the deal with all these mirrors on the walls?" I ask as we make our way through the maze of machines, trying to ignore the grunts and groans and shrieks of those being tortured.

"They're there so you can watch yourself while you work out."

"If you need to work out, I wouldn't think you'd want to look at yourself."

"Some people," he says primly, giving me a look that clearly says that I wouldn't be one of those people, "like to watch their progress as they work their muscles."

"Ah," I say. "I see." I decide not to voice my opinion that the mirrors are also there so that some people can check out how snazzy they look in their fashionable workout togs.

Instead, I ask, "Is there a minimum dollar amount you must spend on your clothes to work out here?" Igor pretends not to hear me.

"Ah, here we are," he says as he stops at a rack of weights. Is that a smirk on his face?

He picks up a couple of dumbbells. "Here, hold these like this, and lift them just so." He hands them to me.

It feels like he's handed me a Volkswagen. I struggle to keep from dropping the damn things on my feet, which do not need to be any flatter than they already are, thank you very much. "You want me," I say through gritted teeth, "to *lift* these?"

Igor is definitely smirking now. "Absolutely."

"More than once?"

"Twelve times. Each."

I consider hefting one, braining him and making a dash for the exit. This is too much. No way can I do this. It hurts; I can feel my muscles screaming in agony already. No way can I come into this place regularly and torture myself, simply to shed a few pounds and to keep from gasping like a fish out of water every time I try to play with my kids. No way.

Igor looks at me expectantly. I look at the weights in my hands. I sigh. Slowly, I begin.

38 - Fighting the War on Flab

I'm hungry.

Actually, ravenous is a more accurate description. Famished. In need of mass quantities of sustenance.

Obviously, I'm on a diet.

I used to sneer at the thought of dieting. In my youth, I could eat whatever I wanted, and in whatever quantities, and hardly gain an ounce. Ah, those were the days....

One of the many mysteries of aging is how your body changes. Rarely is this for the better. In women, the body begins to, well, sag as gravity has its inexorable way, and extra flesh seems to settle in the thigh and upper hindquarter areas. In men, that flesh settles in around the waist region, and that washboard stomach transmutes into love handles, a paunch, a spare tire, or a quivering, jiggling belt buckle-obliterating avalanche in waiting.

For most of us, those extra pounds just seem to appear one day, almost as though we've grown another body part – or lost some. You look down one day and, hey, where did my feet go? They were there yesterday.

And we become adept at making excuses why we don't lose those added pounds. "Gosh, honey," you might say, "these pants sure did shrink when you washed them." Or, in autumn, we might say of the extra flesh: "It's just a little bit of insulation for the cold of winter." Of course, we all know what that really means: I'll be covering up all this flab in layers of puffy clothing for the next several months, so nobody will be able to see all this lard.

But then spring comes and it's time to put on shorts and T-shirts and ... suddenly your body is not a sight that small children and the faint of heart should see. You think about your next trip to the beach, and visions spring to mind of albino hippos wallowing in the shallows as curious sunbathers point and stare.

So you diet. It's no easy thing to change your eating habits and to eat less than the ample quantities to which most of us are accustomed. Besides, we are a nation of eaters. Snacking is practically a national pastime. We're not like other countries where people often go for days between meals. The average American can't go more than an hour or two before they're starving. Not merely hungry, mind you, but simply starving to death.

But it's not all our fault (even though rationalizations are a sure sign that you're about to justify eating that piece of cake). Television is constantly extolling the virtues of attractive humanity as being slim and buff, yet all the while blathering on about all this food you need to eat. Mostly junk food. Our modern society practically forces food down our collective throats. We're all too busy hustling and bustling around to take the time to eat balanced meals, so we end up with fast food. And what are their choices?

"You want fries with that?"

"Um, sure, I guess." You didn't really, since you're trying to lose a little weight, but you don't want to be argumentative.

"You want to jumbo-size that order?"

"I beg your pardon?"

"Jumbo-size. You know, bigger. You can get your order in regular, large, gargantuan, and mammoth."

"Um, just the regular, I think."

"You know, it's only 50 cents more to jumbo-size your order. You'd be a moron not to."

"OK. Sure. I guess." I mean, I wouldn't want someone who works the microphone at a drive-through to think I'm stupid.

"You want pie, cobbler, brownie, cookie or a double-chocolate fudge sundae made with real virtual ice cream with that? They come in 12 sizes."

And so it goes. I asked my doctor how I could lose a little weight. He tells me to eat less and exercise more. This, of course, is advice that is exactly opposite of what I want to hear. I want a diet where I can eat more and exercise less. But not to worry: There are plenty of diet experts out there who will be happy to tell you what you want to hear.

The choices of diet plans are mind-boggling. Clearly, dieting is big business in America. So, how do you choose? How do you decide what is right for you? Low-fat, low-carb, high-protein, good fat and bad fat – I don't want a degree in nutrition, I just want to lose a couple of pounds. I figure I need some guidance. I call the government.

"Hello, Fat Loss Advisory Board."

"Um, did you know..."

"We prefer that you not use the acronym, sir."

"Sure. I was calling because I'm trying to lose some weight."

"Yeah, you and half of America."

"See here. I came to you because you're a government agency. You're supposed to be public servants. You're supposed to exist to help us citizens."

"How very droll, sir."

"I was hoping you could help me make some sense about all these diet plans. I was hoping you had some suggestions."

"Of course, sir. I'll be happy to send you our free pamphlet, 'Trim the Fat the Government Way: Give Us All Your Money So You Can't Afford to Buy Any Food.'"

"Seems rather extreme. I was thinking more along the lines of some of those diet shakes that are so popular. What do you know about them?"

"That if you can stand the idea of drinking most of your food for the next several months you no doubt will drop a few pounds."

"Really?"

"Absolutely. A strawberry shake for breakfast, no matter how delicious, begins to lose a bit of its attraction after about the 18th consecutive morning, so eventually you'll be too sick to want to eat anything."

"Ah. I see. What about these weight-loss programs I see that promise to make you lose 25 pounds in a month but let you eat all you want?"

"Hmmm. I'd say that's an either-or type situation."

"Either or?"

"Yes. Either the company also peddles swamp land for retirement homes or it runs a work farm where you sweat for 20 hours a day at manual labor and eat gruel."

"Oh. What about some of these pills I keep hearing about? The ones that boost your metabolism or curb your appetite?"

"Oh, yes, let's wean ourselves off food so we can become addicted to drugs."

"Pretty cynical, aren't you?"

"Hey, it's the diet business. What can I say?"

"So, I should just follow my doctor's advice?"

"What's that, get a second job so you can afford his bill?"

"Hey, I didn't know bureaucrats had a sense of humor."

"Who's laughing?"

"Well, my doctor says to eat less and exercise more."

"Hmmm. Could work."

"Except the only problem is that it seems as though I can starve myself for days, and then all I have to do is look at a potato chip and I gain five pounds."

"That is a problem. Why not try eating some of that low-calorie food? And they say those diet soft drinks taste just like the regular sodas."

"Only if the regular sodas taste like sponge squeezings. It seems as though any food that is supposed to be good for you tastes so bland it's like they sucked all the flavor out of it."

"That's how it works. Who wants to eat if the food is so bland? Of course, it you really want to lose weight, your doctor is right: You have to exercise more."

"Hey, I exercise."

"Sir, waddling from the couch to the dining room table once a day does not count as exercise."

"That's a cheap shot. Say, just out of curiosity, how much do you weigh?"

"That, sir, is classified information."

"Right. Does that mean you're in the lard-bucket classification, then?"

"Oh, look. It's time for my break. I really must hang up, now."

"Fine by me. I think I'll go and grab me a carrot stick."

"That's the spirit, sir."

"Yeah. Actually, I may jumbo-size this carrot stick. All the way up to a pizza. I'll diet some more tomorrow."

39 - Seeing Straight

A lot of people can't see the forest for the trees. I've had to wear glasses since the fifth grade to see the forest but I could always see the trees up close just fine. Until lately, when they, too, started to get a little blurry.

I remember with depressing clarity the day I got my first pair of glasses. Other than the fact that I got to miss school, I dreaded the whole experience. I could easily envision the taunts of "four-eyes" from my less politically correct classmates, not to mention a lifetime of having an unwieldy apparatus stuck to my face. The gain of clearer eyesight did not seem to balance the negatives for a shy and self-conscious child.

But I endured that trauma and I can't help but think back to that time as I become increasingly aware that after years of dealing with nearsightedness, I'm having trouble reading the fine print now as well. I began noticing that, as I was writing checks in stores, the date on my watch had mysteriously shrunk. I had to squint to see what day of the week it was.

Then there were those times when I'd be reading a piece of paper and realize that I was moving it back and forth in front of me trying to bring it into focus. I felt like I was practicing the trombone.

But the worst part about the whole vision thing to me is that I love to read, especially in bed. The problem is that the combination of tired eyes at night and less-than-brilliant lighting causes complications.

I started out by squinting slightly, but my wife kept asking me why I was lying there making faces. Then I found that if I moved my glasses down a bit on my nose I could focus on the pages better. While my eyes welcomed the improved view, my nose eventually began to complain; something about uncomfortable pinching and blocking of the air passages. Honestly, noses can be such whiners sometimes.

I tried reading without my glasses on at all, but wound up with the book two inches from my face. I don't recommend this, since your arms get tired and the pages keep slapping you in the face every time you turn them.

It's almost enough to make you give up reading and turn on the television, which to anyone interested in stimulation is like passing up the chocolate decadence for dessert in favor of the lime Jell-O.

As I contemplate my dilemma one night, I consider one other possibility. My wife has a couple of old pairs of those reading glasses you can buy in the drugstore, so I scrounge up a pair. I reason that since I can see objects close at hand without my regular glasses, all I need is a pair of those magnifying lenses to sharpen the vision. I try them on, and the world goes blurry. I slide them up and down my nose, and my vision goes from blurry to blurrier to I-think-I-might-be-sick.

Then a brainstorm hits. How about wearing both sets of glasses at the same time? So I put on my glasses over the reading glasses – you kind of have to perch them on top of each other. Voila! The words in my book do the proverbial jumping off the page thing. This is great! This is fabulous! I turn to my wife excitedly.

"Honey," she says, looking at me. "You look ridiculous."

Only slightly deflated, I shrug off her fashion criticism. I can see! I can read! Go ahead, call me six-eyes, I don't care. Of course, I think I'm starting to get a headache, but hey, I can read again. All right, that's definitely a headache coming on, but at least I'm reading. My eyes are starting to ask am I really expecting them to focus on all these distorted images coming in through all those lenses, but this is a really good book and I think I'll just put it down for now and take off all these glasses and turn out the light and see if my head will quit pounding.

I limp along like this for a few weeks, and then one night my wife makes the Dreaded Suggestion:

"Honey, why don't you try some bifocals?"

I turn to look at her and put on a pitying smile.

"Because," I say, not unkindly as I state the obvious, "I don't need bifocals."

"Yes, you do," she declares, unconcerned with the obvious.

"No, I don't," I say, a bit more firmly.

"Do, too."

"Do not."

"Do, too."

"Do not. Do not. Do not! Look, dear, I'm an adult and therefore perfectly capable of making these decisions in a mature and, er, adult manner."

"Yes, and you're getting to be an older adult."

144

"Am not."

"Are, too."

"Am not."

She sniffs and goes back to her book. Sheesh, and they say men act immaturely. You try to conduct a serious conversation with somone....

In my heart of hearts I know, however, that she is right. But everyone I've known with bifocals, including my wife, has struggled mightily to adjust to them. I've heard them grouse and gripe and complain endlessly as they try to look through the right part of the lens to see something close up or far away. I'm not prepared for such a major midlife change.

And to be honest it's more than that. The thing is, bifocals are for, well, not to put too fine a point on it, for old people. They push you right away up a bracket or two into geezerhood. One day you're going along looking at the world through snazzy spectacles, and the next day you're making a spectacle of yourself as your head bobs and weaves while you peer out murkily from behind these clunky two-way windows trying to focus on something, on anything. Can a hearing aid and a walker be far behind?

Before I head down the road toward old age, I ponder my alternatives. I could get contact lens for my near-sightedness and then wear reading glasses for close-up work. I've never worn contact lens, though, because I can't stand to have things near my eyes, such as my fingers trying to put in those itty-bitty pieces of plastic. Plus, I wonder, how do you adapt to not having glasses on after a lifetime of wearing them? I mean, glasses are kind of like windshields for your eyes, keeping all the stray objects in the air like dust and grit and bugs from smacking into your eyeballs as you move along. I don't know about going around without any sort of ocular protection.

Then, of course, there's all the paraphernalia that comes with contact lens, and the distressing amount of time putting them in and taking them out. I'm the type of person who begrudges the time it takes to shave every day; am I going to have the patience to pop things in and out of my eyes all the time? After all, it takes very little effort to put on and take off a pair of glasses.

And what about the reading-at-night problem? There I am, happily reading in bed with my contacts and reading glasses, nodding off. I take off the glasses and turn out the light … and remember I have to get up and go poke around in my eyes before I can go to sleep.

So I rule out contacts. Another possibility is laser surgery. I know they're doing all kinds of wonderful things to eyes with lasers; you can correct either near- or farsightedness in most people. So I could correct my nearsightedness and just go with the reading glasses. Except I don't need any kind of glasses to see how much the surgery costs.

So it's gotta be bifocals. I trudge to my eye doctor's office to officially get the bad news. He confirms my self-diagnosis. He says it won't be too bad. He says they've made all sorts of technological advances in bifocals, that they don't even have lines on the glasses anymore. He says I'll get used to them. Hah! And my wife said I'd get used to having kids around the house, too.

I drag my wife with me to the eyeglass store because, after all, I can't very well see myself when I try on glasses that I can't see out of. I glumly pick out a pair and only half listen as I'm told how wonderful bifocals are.

Days later I go back to pick them up. The big day. Hooray. I feel as though I'm back in the fifth grade. I've been practicing rolling my eyes around and tilting my head up and down, just to get ready. I have a bottle of aspirin with me for the headache I'm sure will come.

I sigh as I take off my regular glasses for the last time; I feel like an old friend is deserting me. I swallow and close my eyes as I try on my brand new bifocals. Slowly, I open my eyes.

Everything looks normal. I look around. Everything is still normal. I glance down. I can read the writing on a piece of paper. I didn't even move my head. I try it again. I can read. I look up. I can see. I look down. I can read. I look up. I can see.

I smile as I walk out of the store and into the world. Everything looks clean and clear and bright. What a great day.

I think I'll head to the bookstore.

40 - *The Older We Get...*

What I want to know is why I'm shorter than I used to be but weigh a whole lot more.

I mean, what's the deal with that? As kids, we put on the pounds as we grew taller. You fill in here, you fill in there, and pretty soon you have an adult-sized body. Growth is replaced by stability. But then, all of a sudden, your body seems to go into reverse.

Take your height. Am I the only person who seems to be shrinking? When I shop for a pair of pants now I buy them an inch shorter than the ones I bought 10 years ago. The odd thing is, I have to buy shoes a size bigger than I used to. From what I can tell, my feet are flattening out. I seem to have better balance now, but every now and then I feel the urge to quack.

These conditions are due, naturally, to the effects of gravity, the irresistible force that results in a general settling of the body. All those brain cells, for instance, that I destroyed and otherwise wasted in my youth have now settled down there around the waist area. Almost all my spare weight is stored in this handy wraparound compartment, sort of a money bag of lard conveniently located next to the stomach.

The rest of the body doesn't seem to take on fat so much as simply sag. Nothing's quite as tight and trim as it used to be. Women, being better at most things in life than men, as a rule are naturally superior saggers. Something to do with chromosomes, no doubt.

Everything tends to even out, however, because men are stuck with the hair thing. Nature tends to redistribute hair on men's body, kind of like an efficient hair recycling system - waste not, want not. Have you ever noticed that as hairlines steadily recede, hair starts sprouting in unlikely places?

It's not something we in polite society talk about, but those of a less refined upbringing no doubt are going around thinking thoughts such as: "Excuse me, sir, but I believe there is a muskrat nesting in your nose." Or, "Pardon me, sir, but a squirrel seems to be stuck in your ear."

So why don't barbers and hairdressers start appealing to the aging Baby Boomer market by offering free hair cuts (hey, they're just going to trim the sides, since that's all there is anyway) with any ear or nose hair cut. This is work more delicate than arranging those three six-foot long strands of hair around a shiny noggin in a failing effort to convince the world that your head doesn't really look like a baboon's butt. Perhaps we could start a fad: You know, styled ear hair, say, or dyed nose hair. How about braided eyebrows? We'll show those young punk kids with their rings stuck everywhere a thing or two about fashion sense.

But all this aging stuff can be depressing. What do we have to look forward to, anyway? Oh, sure, you can try to keep the old body fit and trim, but it's a losing battle. Things will keep wearing out and breaking down. The warranty on certain parts will expire, and they simply won't work properly any more.

That's when we'll all be sitting around complaining and whining and occasionally bragging about bodily functions - kind of like when we were parents for the first time. Only instead of our brand new babies we'll be talking about ourselves.

"Yep," one of us will say, "had a really successful trip to the bathroom this morning. I mean REALLY successful" and the rest of us will be muttering about what a lucky old fart he or she is. Or: "Hey, I ate some real food for breakfast; had me a chocolate donut instead of that gruel I always eat. 'Course, I'll be paying for it later, if you know what I mean." And of course we'll all know what it means. Bathrooms will be the most important rooms in our lives.

So what's a body to do?

Actually, when I get to my golden years, I plan on fighting back. For one thing, I plan on taking up all my old vices again. Smoking, drinking, carousing, partying, leaving the toilet seat up … hey, who cares at that point? I say be who you really want to be without worrying about what anyone else at the retirement home thinks.

That's the ticket. For once in your life, be yourself. Be who you always wanted to be. Act the way you always wanted to act. Even if your body doesn't always work the way it used to, that doesn't mean you have to act your age.

In fact, why wait for old age? The trick to life is to act young, feel young, be young. The sooner you start living young the better.

I intend to get on it right after my nap.